Creativity
in the Primary
Curriculum

Related Titles of Interest

Literacy through Creativity, Prue Goodwin, ISBN: 1–84312–087–9

The Articulate Classroom, Prue Goodwin, ISBN: 1–85346–703–0

Creativity
in the Primary
Curriculum

Edited by Russell Jones and Dominic Wyse

David Fulton Publishers

David Fulton Publishers
2 Park Square, Milton Park, Abingdon, Oxon OX14 4RN

270 Madison Avenue, New York, NY 10016

First published in Great Britain in 2004 by David Fulton Publishers
Reprinted 2005
Transferred to digital printing

David Fulton Publishers is an imprint of the Taylor & Francis Group, an informa business

Copyright © Russell Jones, Dominic Wyse and individual contributors 2004

British Library Cataloguing in Publication Data
A catalogue record for this book is available from the British Library.

ISBN 1 85346 871 1

Typeset by RefineCatch Limited, Bungay, Suffolk

Contents

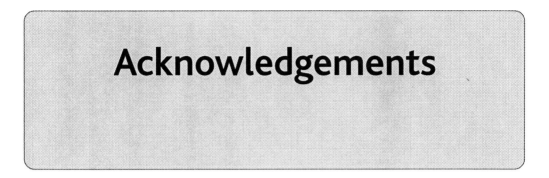

Acknowledgements

Russell and Dominic would both like to thank key staff at Fulton for their guidance and support in the production of this book.

Russell would like to dedicate this book to Billy Cooper.

Dominic looks forward to creative projects with Pasc.

Contributor Biographies

Ruth Adkins began dancing with Cheshire Dance Workshop, as part of various Youth Dance groups and went on to teach contemporary dance workshops and summer schools in primary schools and community groups in Cheshire and Manchester.

John Airs is an educational drama teacher/lecturer working in North West universities, colleges and schools. He works with teachers, students and children on learning in and through the art form of drama. His main publications are *Taking Time To Act*, *Key Ideas in Drama*, and *Speaking, Listening and Drama* (Yrs 1&2, 3&4, 5&6), all with Chris Ball, and *Theatre in Education: Performing for You.*

Jo Dennis attended Nottingham University where she gained a BA (Hons.) in Geography with subsidiary American Literature. She worked in the Health Service for nine years before entering teaching, and gained her MEd in 2000 from Liverpool University. She has worked as a County Tutor for ICT and now teaches in Brookside Primary School in Cheshire where she is ICT and Geography Co-ordinator.

Una Hanley works in the Mathematics Centre at Manchester Metropolitan University. Both as a practitioner in primary classrooms and as an advisory teacher for Mathematics in Salford she was interested in the ways in which children engage with Mathematics rather than just 'do it'. Her recently achieved PhD has led her into further studies into narrative research voices.

Linda Harris has been teaching for 33 years in inner-city Liverpool. She is currently the Deputy Head and Year 6 teacher of Whitefield Primary School. She has always had a special interest in broadening children's experiences and seeking to develop their creativity, particularly through drama.

Helen Hilditch has taught in Cheshire for 21 years and as Deputy Headteacher at Sandiway Primary School for the past 14 years. Prior to her appointment as Deputy Headteacher she was seconded as an advisory teacher working for the Rural Schools' Programme. As part of her wider professional development, Helen has completed a Best Practice Research Scholarship on Creativity and Role Play. She has recently conducted a series of guest lectures on Creativity at Manchester Metropolitan University.

Matthew Hopper is a senior lecturer in the School of Education at Liverpool John Moores University. The main focus of his work is initial teacher education and continuing professional development in the field of Design and Technology. In addition to these core activities Matthew also makes a contribution to a diverse range of both undergraduate and postgraduate programmes including Product Design, Childhood Studies, Information and Communication Technology, and Education Studies. His current research interests include a study of the place of creativity within the curriculum at Key Stages 1 and 2.

Russell Jones is a Senior Lecturer in English and Childhood Studies at Manchester Metropolitan University. He has lectured in English, Drama, Visual Arts, History and Creative Writing. His PhD research was published in the book *Teaching Racism*, and he co-wrote *Teaching English Language and Literacy* with Dominic Wyse. His current interests are in the rights of the child and further developing notions of creative approaches to the teaching of literacy.

Carole Mindham has taught primary children from Nursery to Year 6 in a wide assortment of schools in London, Manchester and Cheshire. She is now Senior Lecturer in Primary Education at Manchester Metropolitan University. Her research work and publications have been within the fields of Peer Assessment and young children's understanding of money and shopping. She is particularly interested in developing creativity through cross-curricular approaches in the primary school and has used her PhD research to encourage the recognition of multiple intelligences.

Ivy Roberts taught in primary schools in Cheshire for 14 years, seven of which were as a primary school head teacher. She has been senior lecturer in Art Education and Professional Studies at Manchester Metropolitan University since 1989. She is the co-author of *Co-ordinating Art Across the Primary School* and now prepares postgraduate and primary initial teacher education students to teach art in primary schools.

David Spendlove is Lecturer in Technology Education at the University of Manchester, having previously been a senior teacher and head of department. He has published widely, and is regarded nationally for his work on CAD/CAM, teaching and learning, educating boys and creativity. In addition, David is a member of the editorial board for the *Journal of Design and Technology Education*, Co-Editor of the International Design and Technology Education Research Conference publication, director of the Design and Technology Association (DATA) and a consultant to QCA and Merseyside Creative Partnerships.

Jill Wright has been a teacher in Liverpool for 13 years and is currently the English and assessment co-ordinator at Whitefield Primary School, Everton. She is a leading literacy teacher and an AST, specialising in the teaching of English. She has also written part of the Cornerstones for Writing scheme for Cambridge University Press.

Dominic Wyse is a Reader in Primary Education. His book, written with Russell Jones, called *Teaching English, Language and Literacy* (RoutledgeFalmer) has proved to be very influential. He is also author of *Becoming a Primary Teacher* (RoutledgeFalmer). Dominic is currently managing, with David Spendlove, a large creativity research project funded by Merseyside Creative Partnerhips. His recent research articles have provided a critique of government policy on the teaching of English at primary school level. His most recent book is *Childhood Studies: An Introduction* (Blackwell Publishers).

Introduction

People are attracted to teaching for a variety of reasons, but chief among these are wanting to 'make a difference', wanting to 'inspire' and wanting to 'capture pupils' imaginations'. New teachers are hopeful that they have the ability to turn interest into passion, to turn ability into talent and to turn good ideas into achievement. This is the excitement and enthusiasm that the Department for Education and Skills (DfES) implied with its 'Can you start a fire?' campaign for the next generation of entrants into the teaching profession.

Words like inspiration, imagination, excitement and enthusiasm are perfectly supported by creative primary teaching. You might think that this is obvious, but a very important report called *All Our Futures* (National Advisory Committee on Creative and Cultural Education (NACCCE) 1999) has resulted in much discussion about the place of creativity in the modern primary curriculum. The report quoted Einstein, who claimed that 'Imagination is more important than knowledge', and suggested that this could be helped to flourish if the six principles on which the curriculum should be based are adopted:

- Breadth
- Balance
- Relevance
- Parity
- Entitlement
- Access

(NACCCE 1999: 84)

The report called for a greater balance between the emphasis on different subjects in the curriculum: 'In order to achieve parity, the existing distinction between core and foundation subjects should be removed' (p. 87). Unfortunately, this recommendation was not followed when the National Curriculum 2000 was put into place. Perhaps we shouldn't be surprised when we look at the events surrounding the publication of *All Our Futures*. The report was released to the press at 5pm on a Friday afternoon when Professor Robinson (the lead author) was out of the country. There were problems with locating copies, and early enquiries were met with the answer that the report was already 'out of print'. The government declined to comment on all the positive feedback the document attracted from teachers' and head teachers' associations (Gold 2000).

Although *All Our Futures* has had only a limited effect on policy for older children, there is evidence that the youngest children may have benefited: 'There is a strong case for a more developed provision for creative and cultural education in early years education' (NACCCE 1999: 76). The young child has an enormous capacity to learn in a vast range of areas and in many different ways, but if these capacities are not used they are allocated (cognitively) to other things. This means that there is a danger that the facility could be lost. The broad themes of the *Curriculum Guidance for the Foundation Stage* (Qualifications and Curriculum Authority (QCA) 2000), including the one called 'Creative Development', are a welcome addition to the statutory curriculum.

All Our Futures is only one recent, but significant, development in thinking about creativity. However, to introduce the subject of the book properly we need to address some of the history of developments in creativity research, theory and practice.

Defining creativity

According to psychologists the modern era for creativity research began following J. P. Guildford's address to the American Psychological Association in 1949. He argued that, up to that point, researchers had emphasised convergent thinking skills and had ignored divergent thinking skills. The use of the word 'creativity' in the title of the presentation and subsequent paper was used to sum up the kind of divergent thinking that he had in mind. In 1957 the Soviets launched the first artificial space satellite and the Americans saw a lack of creativity as one of the reasons for their failure to win the first event in the space race (Cropley 2001). This had the effect of galvanising the field of creativity research.

In 1961, Rhodes (as cited in Feldhusen and Goh 1995) defined creativity as consisting of a process, a product, a person and a situation. Some writers refer to the situation or the context for the creativity as environmental 'press' (meaning influence) which has resulted in the shorthand version: the '4 Ps' of creativity – process, product, person and press. Mackinnon's well-known definition of creativity also emphasises the end-product or response:

> It involves a response or an idea that is novel or at the very least statistically infrequent. But novelty or originality of thought or action, while a necessary aspect of creativity, is not sufficient. If a response is to lay claim to being part of the creative

process, it must to some extent be adaptive to, or of, reality. It must serve to solve a problem, fit a situation, or accomplish some recognizable goal. And thirdly, true creativeness involves sustaining of the original insight, an evaluation and elaboration of it, a developing of it to the full. Creativity, from this point of view, is a process extended in time and characterized by originality, adaptiveness, and realization.

(*op. cit.*: 233)

Psychological research through the 1970s and 1980s was largely concerned with more detailed attempts to define, and ultimately measure, creativity. The Torrance tests of creativity were one of the most well-known examples of such measurement, but like so many standardised tests they came under increasing criticism due to the telling argument that creativity was much more complex than even these well-thought-through tests were showing. As a result, the most recent research has shown some lines of enquiry that are of particular use to practitioners.

Csikszentmihályi (1990) advanced the significant idea that creativity is not an individual attribute but a product of societal judgements which involves interaction among a domain (opportunities and constraints), a person and a field (specialists). A programme of research advanced by Amabile (1990: 65) has assessed creativity by asking participants to create products and then having expert judges rate the creativity of the outcomes: 'A product or response is creative to the extent that appropriate observers independently agree it is creative. Appropriate observers are those familiar with the domain in which the product was created or the response articulated.' These promising lines of thinking are part of the reason that Vernon's definition (1989: 94) is widely welcomed: 'Creativity means a person's capacity to produce new or original ideas, insights, restructurings, inventions, or artistic objects, which are accepted by experts as being of scientific, aesthetic, social, or technological value.'

The move away from defining creativity as a fixed entity to one which is dependent upon people's judgements is important for teachers because they are often in the role of assessing the extent to which school work is creative. Teachers are both experts in their subjects studied at degree level and beyond, and experts in child development, which gives them significant expert knowledge to judge the creativity of children's work. This may not give them the expertise to judge what Cropley (2001) calls 'sublime' creativity, but it does give them the expertise to judge 'everyday' or 'little c' (Craft 2000) creativity.

Teaching creativity

There are hundreds of programmes that claim to enhance children's creative development. These range from detailed approaches carried out over quite lengthy periods of time to specific techniques such as SCAMPER, which is used to change something that already exists to produce novelty by Substituting, Combining, Adapting, Magnifying, Putting to a different use, Eliminating and Rearranging/Reversing (Cropley 2001). Another example is the use of brain-storming, which has been extended to include more structured ways of generating ideas such as mind maps and other visual techniques which use hierarchies of categories. Many of the packages begin their lives in the business sector, such as Edward de Bono's lateral thinking approach. However, in spite of great interest in the area and much financial success for some approaches, there is a lack of empirical evidence: 'A clear, unequivocal, and incontestable answer to the question of how creativity can be enhanced is not to be found in the psychological literature' (Nicholson 1999: 407).

At the current time various publications are offering suggestions as to how the theory of multiple intelligences can be used in the classroom. Links are also frequently being made between multiple intelligence approaches and creativity. While it is true that the divergent thinking has been recognised as being part of creative minds, this is only one part of what is required to be creative.

Despite the lack of evidence about general approaches to teaching creativity, progress continues to be made in relation to the many aspects that contribute to creative development. Amabile has produced much useful research which, as we saw earlier, has helped us to understand that definitions of creativity must take into account the fact that this is a socially constructed concept dependent upon the judgement of observers. She has also reported work (Amabile 1985) which found that when a questionnaire which focused on intrinsic motivation was given to some students prior to writing a poem, this subsequently resulted in more creative poems (as assessed by 12 practising poets) than the group who were given a questionnaire which focused upon extrinsic motivation. One of the implications of this research, which confirms other theoretical work, is that teachers' attempts to engage children's motivation through intrinsic rewards are worth pursuing.

Overall, researchers remain optimistic that creativity can be enhanced by the ways that teachers work with pupils and students. A number of factors have been identified that necessitate the need to

- support domain-specific-knowledge: pupils need to understand as much as possible about the domain (often the subject area) in which they are doing the creative work;
- reward curiosity and exploration;
- build motivation, particularly internal motivation;
- encourage risk-taking;
- have high expectations/beliefs about creative potential of students: this applies to both teachers' views of their pupils and pupils' own self-image;

- give opportunities for choice and discovery:

  The evidence is fairly compelling, and not surprising, that people are more interested in – more internally motivated to engage in – activities they have chosen for themselves than activities that have been selected for them by others, or in which they are obliged to engage for reasons beyond their control. (Dudek and Côté 1994; Kohn 1993);

- develop students' self-management skills.

  (Nicholson 1999: 409)

The point about opportunities for choice is highly significant, and one which the English education system has repeatedly neglected, particularly since 1988.

In summary, the research shows us that something is creative if it is

- novel;

- created with an understanding of the field;

- valued as creative by observers.

We can apply these characteristics of creativity to this book. The book is novel because it clearly addresses most of the subjects in the primary curriculum in a subject specific way. Many other good books on the subject of creativity tend to take themes as their organising structure. This is helpful in emphasising the cross-curricular nature of much creative practice but perhaps lacks the necessary clear focus on practice within a subject which is still the dominant organisational structure in schools. This reflects a practical reality that we all have to face, although it is a curriculum structure of which we remain critical. All the contributors have expertise in their subjects and the field of primary education, a necessary precondition for creativity. We leave it to our readers (the observers) to decide whether the book really does make a creative contribution.

This book invites you to think creatively about your own potential and practice. Each chapter has been written as a result of close collaboration between practising teachers, advisers and academics. At a time when the curriculum has never been more restrictive and (potentially) mechanistic, the authors have found ways to bring enthusiasm and excitement into the classroom. Each chapter contains one or more case studies which describe exactly how creative classrooms operate: the role of the child, the characteristics of the outcomes and the reasoning of the teacher. Interview data are included to enable you to 'hear' the teacher's voice explaining their ideas and decision-making processes.

While researching this book we quickly realised that the successful lessons being described were ones where current prescribed practice was overturned. The most creative lessons were ones where there was a different kind of relationship in the classroom, one that was not about an authoritative figure who held answers, resources and power, but one which was based on mutual respect, trust and, above all, enquiry. These classrooms asked questions of themselves. Pupils were not afraid to ask the question, 'Wouldn't it be more interesting if we did it this way?', and teachers were not afraid to work with these suggestions. In the environments where creativity flourished it was not because the teachers had carefully organised a creative slot in the term's curriculum; it was because creative approaches and possibilities underpinned the relationship between teachers and learners and the culture of the classroom.

One of the other main features of the book is the recurrent description of the obvious barriers to creativity that teachers in all subjects continue to wrestle with in England. The blame for this can be laid squarely at the door of educational policy since 1997. As we explained earlier, *All Our Futures* sent a powerful message about the importance, and neglect, of creativity. The possibility of a new government strategy on primary education in 2003 raised many people's hopes.

The primary strategy

Excellence and Enjoyment: A Strategy for Primary Schools (Department for Education and Skills (DfES) 2003) was the third major national strategy during the period from 1997 to 2003. It came on top of an unprecedented number of government interventions in primary education. In spite of teachers' feelings of 'intervention overload', it was anticipated keenly as there had been growing consensus that educational policy in England was too prescriptive and that this was impacting negatively on things like creative teaching and creative learning. It was hoped that fundamental reforms might result in a more appropriate level of professional autonomy for teachers including the opportunity to teach more creatively with fewer constraints. The primary strategy document does indeed include words like 'freedom' and 'empowerment', and on page 18, for the first time, after the executive summary, the word 'creativity' appears:

> 2.11 Some teachers question whether it is possible to exercise their curricular freedom, because of the priority the Government attaches to improving literacy and numeracy. But as OfSTED reports have shown, it is not a question of 'either', 'or'. Raising standards and making learning fun can and do go together. The best primary schools have developed timetables and teaching plans that combine creativity with strong teaching in the basics.
>
> (DfES 2003: 18)

This paragraph does clearly identify an aspect of the debate, but it is too simplistic. It is true that it is not impossible to teach creatively and to help children learn creatively in spite of government constraints, but this misses the real point, which is: is the primary strategy the best way to achieve creativity?

A significant problem which remains is the continued emphasis on the literacy strategy which, despite optimistic expectations of a quickened death, still looms large in the primary strategy. One of the general consequences of this is the addition of yet another layer of bureaucracy to the literacy strategy which was already too bureaucratic. On the one hand we are told: 'The National Literacy and Numeracy Strategies, though they are supported strongly, are *not statutory* [emphasis added] and can be adapted to meet schools' particular needs' (*ibid.*: 16). But, on the other hand,

> The Literacy and Numeracy Strategies have, according to all those who have evaluated them, been strikingly successful at improving the quality of teaching and raising standards in primary schools. But we need to *embed the lessons of the National Literacy and Numeracy Strategies more deeply* [emphasis added].
>
> (DfES 2003: 27)

The claim that the NLS *Framework for Teaching* has been strikingly successful by all those who have evaluated it is simply not supported by evidence. The government commissioned a team from the University of Toronto to carry out an independent evaluation of the strategies. The first report was lukewarm at best about the impact of the pedagogy of the literacy strategy:

> Clearly it would be naive to conclude that the instructional and other practices included in NLNS were the sole causes of the gains being made [in test results]. For example, as we have discussed in several other sections of this report:
>
> • There is, at best, uneven evidence that such practices can be counted on to 'produce' numeracy and literacy gains . . .
>
> (Earl *et al.* 2000: 36)

The second report affirmed this position by the claim that 'the strategies themselves are a unique blend of practices whose effects, to our knowledge, have never been carefully tested in real field settings' (Earl *et al.* 2001: 81). The idea that the literacy strategy has been completely successful is laid to rest in the final report: 'we recognise . . . that both strategies have been contentious' (Earl *et al.* 2003: 34). Remarkably, even Ofsted, which has relentlessly applied pressure on schools and universities to adopt the pedagogy of the NLS in the past, has recognised that all is not well and has prioritised as its first action point that government should 'undertake a critical review of the NLS, paying particular attention to the clarity and usefulness of the framework as a tool for improving standards in literacy across the whole curriculum (Ofsted 2002: 4). This is something that we have argued for in a number of publications since 2000 (Wyse 2000; Wyse 2001a; Wyse 2001b; Wyse 2003; Wyse and Jones 2001).

The NLS *Framework for Teaching* is too prescriptive and hinders creativity. Its continuing emphasis in the primary strategy is not supported even by the government's own evidence. Evidence that government has responded to the growing complaints about the prescription in the curriculum is shown in the changes of language evident in the primary strategy document but not in substantial action.

There are a number of other barriers that creative teachers have had to undermine and these form a hitlist of things that would have been replaced if we had been responsible for the primary strategy:

1. Testing

Children in England are tested more than children in any other European country. Testing has narrowed the curriculum at the expense of creative teaching and learning. Incontestable evidence that testing has helped raised standards has not been found.

2. The inspection regime

> My two long lives – in education and in art – have left me greatly strengthened in the beliefs which began to dawn on me as a young man. I believe that each one of us is born with creative power, with the attributes of the artist and the craftsman. I believe that the arts must be at the very centre, the core of our lives.
>
> (Tanner 1987: 214)

In the present regime it is hard to believe that the quote above came from a member of Her Majesty's Inspectorate (HMI). HMI became the Office for Standards in Education (Ofsted) and changed from an organisation that was largely independent from government to one which simply enforces the government's latest policy initiative. This change in role has been felt particularly acutely in university education departments responsible for teacher-training. Much as government might like universities to simply obey their pronouncements on teaching and learning, the role of universities to oppose and challenge inadequate policy of all kinds transcends the considerable pressure that continues to be applied to conform. The use of the word 'compliance' since 1998 was a significant change of vocabulary which sums up the view from Ofsted that teacher educators (including teachers in partnership with universities) should simply do as they are told.

The lack of validity (including the lack of transparency) of Ofsted's data-collection methods; the shameful disregard of wider reliable research evidence to guide their pedagogic pronouncements; many primary inspectors' lack of experience in teaching and learning in higher education; dubious reporting revealing weak analysis of data; interrogatory interviewing techniques at the expense of appropriate professional discussion; and the draconian restrictions on the right to reply to verbal feedback and draft inspection reports (and in some cases shocking distortions and unacceptable levels of written English in these reports) reflects a system that is completely incompatible with a democratic society and one which actively discourages creative teaching and learning.

Richards (1999: 144), an ex-senior HMI himself, has claimed that we live in a climate of 'democratic totalitarianism' where the views, needs, experience and recommendations of teachers are systematically ignored in order to adhere to a vision of prescription, measurability, comparability and accountability.

3. Objective-led teaching

There is very little research evidence to support the idea that the best teaching is always dominated by short-term lesson objectives. What the research actually suggests is that good teaching utilises a range of different ways to structure lessons and sequences of lessons. It is also plausible that the use of a range of teaching strategies may benefit pupils' different learning styles. However, much more evidence needs to be collected on the nature of learning styles and the ways that teaching styles might fit with these in spite of the currently fashionable use of multiple intelligence theory.

In view of this lack of evidence it is disappointing that otherwise promising publications seem hampered by the need to enforce the notion of objective-led teaching. A significant report by Ofsted (2003) and a web-based resource offered by the QCA clearly show that creativity is important, but creativity only really counts if 'imaginative activity is purposeful: that is it is directed to achieving an objective', and when 'the outcome must be of value in relation to the objective' (Qualifications and Curriculum Authority 2003: online). In the section titled 'How Can Teachers Promote Creativity?' we are informed that creativity is achieved by 'taking pupils through the creative process step by step'. Genuine creativity has very little to do with the idea of a step-by-step process, as can be seen from the examples in our book.

The views of creative people

Many creative people, for example the award-winning writers Philip Pullman and David Almond, are heavily criticising the English education system:

> There are no rules. Anything that's any good has to be discovered in the process of writing it . . . we cannot require everything to take place under the glare of discussion and checking and testing and consultation: some things have to be private

and tentative. Teaching at its best can give pupils the confidence to discover this mysterious state and to begin to explore the things that can be discovered there.

(Pullman 2003: 2)

Pullman has described the curriculum for young people as 'brutal', suggesting that we are creating a generation of children who hate reading and who 'feel nothing but hostility for literature' (Ward 2003). Five leading children's authors have already voiced their concerns personally to the government and leave readers in little doubt about their dismay about some teaching practices. Anne Fine feels that there has been 'a real drop in the standard of children's writing – not in grammar, construction or spelling, but in the untestable quality of creativity' (Katbamna 2003: 3). Fine no longer judges children's writing competitions and has stated that 'The standards, even of the best, are generally so truly awful that I rarely think we should give a prize at all' (*ibid.*).

The regular *Times Educational Supplement* feature, 'My Best Teacher', is a powerful reminder of the lasting positive influence that really creative teachers have on their pupils. Booker Prize winner Ben Okri used the opportunity to voice his frustration with the education system:

I think the culture of education is wrong. It is too much like a production line – you're doing this so at the end of the day you'll be doing that . . . For the past 10 years I have been trying to find someone to teach me how to swim, and it has led me to thinking that the great problem of teaching is that people have forgotten how to learn. We're not learners any more, we're collectors of facts. People tell me, 'Do it this way, do it that way', and whenever I do, I end up nearly drowning.

(Okri 2000: 7)

Nevertheless, we do not despair. We take the lead from these creative voices and realise that we need to fight for a creative curriculum. This kind of intellectual fight is part of what makes the profession such a fascinating one. The examples in every chapter of this book, of inspirational teachers at work, show that in spite of the many barriers there are growing opportunities for creative teaching and learning. We hope that you will try the many suggestions that are offered and add more of your own so that all our futures will be better.

References

Amabile, T. (1990) 'Within you, without you: the social psychology of creativity and beyond', in M. Runco and R. Albert (eds) *Theories of Creativity*. London: Sage.

Craft, A. (2000) *Creativity Across the Primary Curriculum: Framing and Developing Practice*. London: RoutledgeFalmer.

Cropley, A. J. (2001) *Creativity in Education and Learning: A Guide for Teachers and Educators*. London: Kogan Page.

Csikszentmihályi (1990) 'The domain of creativity', in M. Runco and R. Albert (eds) *Theories of Creativity*. London: Sage.

Department for Education and Skills (DfES) (2003) *Excellence and Enjoyment: A Strategy for Primary Schools*. Nottingham: DfES Publications.

Earl, L., Fullan, M. and Leithwood, K. *et al.* (2000) *Watching and Learning: OISE/UT Evaluation of the Implementation of the National Literacy and Numeracy Strategies*. Nottingham: DfEE Publications.

Earl, L., Fullan, M. and Leithwood, K. *et al.* (2001) *Watching and Learning 2: OISE/UT Evaluation of the implementation of the National Literacy and Numeracy Strategies*. Nottingham: DfEE Publications.

Earl, L., Watson, N., Levin, B. and Leithwood, K. *et al.* (2003) *Watching and Learning 3: Final Report of the External Evaluation of England's National Literacy and Numeracy Strategies*. Nottingham: DfES Publications.

Feldhusen, J. F. and Goh, B. E. (1995) 'Assessing and accessing creativity: an integrative review of theory, research, and development'. *Creativity Research Journal*, **8**: 231–47.

Gold, K. (2000) 'Why I am angry that the government is keeping creativity in the dark: in conversation with Professor Ken Robinson'. *Times Higher Educational Supplement*, 28 January.

Katbamna, M. (2003) 'Crisis of creativity'. *Guardian Education*, 30 September.

National Advisory Committee on Creative and Cultural Education (NACCCE) (1999) *All Our Futures: Creativity, Culture and Education*. Suffolk: DfEE Publications.

Nicholson, R. S. (1999) 'Enhancing creativity', in R. J. Sternberg (ed.) *Handbook of Creativity*. Cambridge: Cambridge University Press.

Ofsted (2002) *The National Literacy Strategy: The First Four Years 1998–2002*. London: Office for Standards in Education.

Ofsted (2003) 'Expecting the unexpected: developing creativity in primary and secondary schools'. London: Ofsted

Okri, B. (2000) 'My best teacher' (in discussion with Hilary Wilce). *Times Educational Supplement* (Friday section), 19 September.

Pullman, P. (2003) 'Lost the plot'. *Guardian Education*, 30 September.

Qualifications and Curriculum Authority (QCA) (2000) *Curriculum Guidance for the Foundation Stage*. London: QCA.

Qualifications and Curriculum Authority (QCA) (2003) National Curriculum in Action. Retrieved (7 November) from www.ncaction.org.uk.

Richards, C. (1999) *Primary Education – At A Hinge of History?* London: Falmer Press.

Ryhammer, L. and Brolin, C. (1999) 'Creativity research: historical considerations and main lines of development'. *Scandinavian Journal of Educational Research*, **43** (3): 259–73.

Tanner, R. (1987) *Double Harness*. London: Impact Books.

Vernon, P. (1989) 'The nature–nurture problem in creativity', in J. Glover, R. Ronning and C. Reynolds (eds) *Handbook of Creativity*. London: Plenum Press.

Ward, L. (2003) 'Tests are making children hate books'. *Guardian Education*, 30 November.

Wyse, D. (2000) 'Phonics: the whole story?: a critical review of empirical evidence'. *Educational Studies*, **26**(3): 355–64.

Wyse, D. (2001a) 'Grammar for writing?: a critical review of empirical evidence'. *British Journal of Educational Studies*, **49** (4): 411–27.

Wyse, D. (2001b) 'Promising yourself to do better?: target-setting and literacy'. *Education 3–13*, **29** (2): 13–18.

Wyse, D. (2003) 'The National Literacy Strategy: a critical review of empirical evidence'. *British Educational Research Journal*, **29** (6).

Wyse, D. and Jones, R. (2001) *Teaching English, Language and Literacy*. London: RoutledgeFalmer.

CHAPTER 1

English

Russell Jones and Dominic Wyse

It is not difficult to argue that English is a creative subject. Imagine your favourite play; take *A Midsummer Night's Dream* for example. Shakespeare's creativity as a writer is continually added to by the creative interpretations of directors, designers and actors. In this case, English shows itself to be a creative subject with aspects of performance art: in America, English is often referred to as a 'language art'. When moulding language the writer creates the text and the reader responds to the message. In doing this the reader applies his/her own interpretation of the text which in itself is a creative process. It is for this reason that the study of literature is so fascinating because people's views of a text vary so widely. All of these elements and more combine to give English its creative character. To confirm this we can also see parallels with other arts subjects. Take music for example. The composer, similar to the writer, creates music, and the performer, rather like the reader, interprets the composer's intentions by creating their own performance.

In order to explore the idea of different responses to text and also to illustrate our conviction that the definition of text includes multimedia images, let us share an anecdote. Dominic first came across *Lord of the Rings* when he was a young teenager. He read about the first 40 pages and found it boring, so went on to read something else. Some 30 years later Dominic's son Oliver asked again and again to see the film of *Lord of the Rings*, so eventually the DVD was bought. This led to a rich seam of development for Oliver: role-play using his bow and arrows, purchased from York's Yorvik Centre, and his Harry Potter sword with sound effects; dramatic re-enactment with toy models of the characters; defeat of Orcs, Uruk-Hai and other unpleasant monsters on the Sony Playstation *Lord of the Rings* game; and all of these in the context of sustained motivation, interest and determination. Oliver also made a very good attempt (for a seven-year-old) to read *The Fellowship of the Ring*, which quite quickly resulted in him skimming and scanning to find his favourite bits.

Dominic's own interest in the book had been rekindled along with a slight guilt that he still hadn't read one of the greatest pieces of literature, so he tried again, and was transfixed. Many interesting conversations followed where father and son compared their understandings of the film version and their different readings of the *Fellowship*. Oliver's factual knowledge of characters and particular details remained higher than his dad's, but because he didn't read all of the *Fellowship* he had less specific evidence of where, for example, the film differed from the books. A case in point is the chapter about Tom Bombadil, which doesn't appear in the film.

By contrast, Russell had read *Lord of the Rings* and his daughter Sophie had also become entranced by *The Fellowship of the Ring* DVD, although her response to this text was quite different. Having watched the film she returned to the scene of Bilbo's 111th birthday party and spent an afternoon learning Frodo's dance, rewinding the film and joining in with the festivities. From there, she completed her usual ritual of selecting sections of dialogue to memorise by heart and then re-enacting them with her own toys. This began with the opening

'You're late!'
'A wizard is never late, Frodo Baggins, and neither is he early. He arrives precisely when he means to.'

and continued through to the complicated scenes prior to the start of the quest, where she spent several days memorising lines and re-enacting them in a clear attempt to grasp and control narrative structure and character motivation. Several questions along the lines of 'Dad, why do they all have more than one name?' reflected her desire for accuracy and appropriateness within her re-enactments.

The many aspects of creativity and learning in these episodes came about due to the excitement and interest generated by a film. The significance of film for both children was one important element of the creativity, but without another element – the freedom to develop their own interests – there would not have been the same level of engagement, nor, arguably, the same level of learning. The anecdote serves to remind us that in the twenty-first century a film and even a video game are just as much a 'text' as a book is.

This whole episode coincided with a paper I was writing about the research base for the literacy strategy and it set my mind thinking about an idea for a new story. The main character will be *Stanno the Grey* (pronounced with a Manchester /o/ perhaps) and the film will be called *Lord of the Ringbinders*. The most important scene toward the end of the film will be when the ring*binder* is finally destroyed!

But Gollum, dancing like a mad thing, held aloft the ring, a finger still thrust within its circle. It shone now as if verily it was wrought of living fire.

'Precious, precious, precious!' Gollum cried. 'My precious! O my precious!' And with that, even as his eyes were lifted up to gloat on his prize, he stepped too far, toppled, wavered for a moment on the brink, and then with a shriek he fell.

(Tolkien 1955: 925)

Oliver and Sophie's experiences illustrate the importance of film, and in particular the learning that occurred through talk and play. Moving image work can offer a natural stimulus for talk; a resource called *Story Shorts*, by the British Film Institute (BFI), is interesting in this respect.

Pilot work for *Story Shorts* involved teachers and others from Birmingham LEA; Bristol and Lambeth EAZ; Bristol Watershed Media Centre; and Warwickshire Arts Zone. Some of the teachers' comments show their excitement about the work: 'I have been more surprised by the children's reactions to the films than anything else I have ever seen.'; 'Using the film *Growing* stimulated the strongest poetry ever written by the children.' The resource consists of a series of films which are about five minutes long. The films are all interesting and the length means that they can be used more easily in a literacy hour than a feature film. However, this does raise some issues. Some of the best work with film can come from using films that are current and that relate closely to children's interests. Although these are feature-length films, DVD technology means that they can be viewed in short sections (called 'chapters'). This means that teachers can design activities which do not require children to see the whole film each time.

Story Shorts suggests a set of opening questions that can be used to stimulate discussion: the '3 Cs' are Camera; Colour; Character; and the '3 Ss' are Story; Sound; Setting. So, for example, with regard to *Lord of the Rings* you might ask: 'What is the motion of the *camera* just before we see an Orc being born from the filth of the earth?' Or, 'What kinds of *colours* do you see after Gandalf's death as the fellowship emerge from the Mines of Moria?' Or, 'What kinds of *sounds* make the black riders so terrifying?' Following whole-group discussion supported by the Cs and Ss questions, there are suggestions for how the films can be used to stimulate other more extended activities which take speaking and listening into writing and drawing.

Story Shorts is more about using film as a stimulus for reflection than about actually getting involved with creating films but there are many examples where the skills learned could be applied to such work. Although it steers an uneasy path through the competing demands of the objectives in the Framework for Teaching and the institute's own agenda for greater knowledge about the techniques of film-making, it is an important development in the context of working with film to support the teaching of English at primary level.

We have highlighted the importance of film to talk and creativity because we think that images are still very underused in primary classrooms. Children's lives are heavily influenced by both still and moving images, and for this reason alone the education system needs to engage with these.

In the introduction to this book we showed how the primary strategy of 2003 represented another in a long line of barriers to teaching creatively. However, this and other difficulties have not stopped talented teachers finding ways to overcome the barriers because of their belief that creativity is too important to be sacrificed for the latest government policy initiative. The following transcript shows how one teacher achieves this:

Russell: We've talked about the kinds of creative things you bring to your teaching, but they have all been related to work outside the classroom, or to creative tasks that you have set as homework. This all seems to happen outside the literacy hour. Is that the case?

Teacher: Well, I've always had the gift of being able to get good writing from children but I couldn't tell anybody how I did it; I thought it was just me and my personality. I'm teaching Y3 now and I have taught reception through to year 6, but I honestly don't think I used to plan enough. I got the results but I didn't know how I got them. The Literacy Strategy made me plan more carefully, I *have* to do it now.

Russell: Can you give me an example?

Teacher: Well, we were doing Native American Indians and we had been looking at dream catchers and we'd talked about Native American Indian life and looked at artefacts. I had to cover 'adjectives' with the NLS, and I thought, 'How can I make this interesting?' I did some modelled writing and we talked about what adjectives are, and we shared all this, and then what I asked them to do was to take photographs and use adjectives. They had to make a list of adjectives that came into their head from the photograph and then put them into their piece of writing, and to me the writing had much more depth than if I'd just given them an exercise out of an exercise book.

Russell: Or if you'd just covered up the adjectives in your big book.

Teacher: Exactly, but then I took it one step further, because we'd been doing *Indian in the Cupboard*, the book. Well, we had a big *papier mâché* Indian in the classroom in the corner and I said that their focus was to write about this Indian in the classroom, and to write about what would happen if he came alive; but I said, 'To make your story more interesting, I want you to be aware of the adjectives you use'. Now my very weakest child came up. She was working towards level 1 in literacy. Well I nearly cried when I read her story; it was just amazing. She had just . . . it gave me goosebumps. Some of this class are quite clever children, they came up on level 3, but for this child not only was the spelling quite good, the structure was there and her use of adjectives was amazing. When I read it out as it should have been read, her face . . . her smile just got bigger and bigger and bigger!

Although the teacher found a way to make the study of adjectives interesting there was much more going on, the things that we think helped to make a good teaching experience: a really good book; recognition that children have to be motivated; use of images and artefacts; a role-play scenario to provide an audience and purpose for the writing; and a fascination about children's language use.

We have known for a long time that good teaching is full of these things and more. Prior to 1997 there was substantial evidence to guide policy-making in terms of the teaching of English, which was largely reflected in the original 1988 National Curriculum English programmes of study, a section of the National Curriculum which achieved a rare amount of consensus for such a controversial area. The NLS *Framework for Teaching* (a very strongly recommended way to deliver reading and writing in the 2000 National Curriculum) quite deliberately broke with the past and pushed several political agendas which have recurred throughout the history of English teaching. The heavy emphasis on phonics in the teaching of reading is one example that continues to be over-emphasised, yet reading creatively requires a very careful balance between maintaining the motivation and creativity of the children and the teacher, and teaching the necessary skills.

Reading

Phonics

In 2000, Dominic carried out an extensive analysis of research on the teaching of phonics. This analysis threw up some interesting findings.

- It is still not clear whether written-word identification is enhanced by phonological knowledge. The question of whether phonological knowledge is acquired simply as a product of greater experience of word identification through reading texts, or whether it helps word identification and is learned in advance, has received different answers from good research.
- There is a lack of research which has looked longitudinally at children's continuing development. The longitudinal research that has been done suggests that phonics teaching is not successful for *all* children.
- There is evidence that children whose phonics teaching is decontextualised from whole texts have less positive attitudes to reading.
- Whole language teaching has had a positive impact on children's motivation.
- Two studies of children who could read *before* they started school noted the rich literate environments of the children and the fact that the children had acquired the necessary phonological knowledge *without* systematic phonics teaching.

- Most of the research on phonics teaching uses statistical analyses of standardised reading test scores as the basis for the claims. These analyses tend to show only marginal gains. They also fail to highlight those individual children in the samples who failed to make improved progress.

Overall, the research findings suggest that the teaching of phonics should be brief, enjoyable and, in the main, aimed at children of age 5–6. The idea that Year 3 and 4 children will benefit from more phonics is not something that is supported by research.

In 2002 the DfES/Harrison published *Roots and Research* which describes itself as an update to *The NLS Review of Research and Related Evidence*. The document contains an extraordinary statement about phonics:

> Recently, we have entered a period of comparative calm in what are sometimes called the reading wars, at least in the UK, and it is noticeable that there has been *a deafening silence from researchers* in relation to the phonics teaching strategy advocated by the NLS. The reason for the silence is clear: researchers agree that the phonics strategy is more or less right, and in the small number of areas of minor disagreement, there isn't really conclusive evidence either way.

CAN YOU HEAR US? – if we may briefly adopt a similarly emotional tone! The words 'deafening silence' gives a clue that this statement is polemical rather than based on a rigorous review of *all* evidence: there is a well-known difference between hearing and listening. A more accurate summary would have resulted from a review of other evidence which does not fit with Harrison's view that the phonics strategy is more or less right. For example, Harrison suggests that a major American government publication (National Reading Panel 2001) gives strong backing to the case for phonics teaching. But Harrison fails to deal with the damning criticisms of the National Reading Panel that Gerald Coles's (2003) book *Reading the Naked Truth* (and many other American publications) convincingly portrays. In the book Coles shows that yet more state-imposed phonics was politically motivated, that the so-called science is flawed and that there are numerous problems with the main studies that became the justification for the National Reading Panel's conclusions. Given that psychological research still seems to be unnaturally influential on English teaching policy, this critique is all the more powerful as it comes from a psychologist.

Phonics teaching and other word-level work should be linked much more closely to real texts that children are reading and writing. As far as reading is concerned, the obvious way to do this is to focus on text-level work as part of shared reading and then to use the same text for word-level work. Let's take *I'm Coming to Get You!* by Tony Ross. I want to put aside, for the purpose of this discussion, the huge range of text-level talk and activities that this book can stimulate, in order to concentrate on the phonological knowledge that might be actively developed simply through discussion about the text. Here are some suggestions for the way we might talk to children if our focus was phonemes and graphemes, presuming text-level discussion had taken place previously:

Can you find two words that begin with the /P/ sound on the first page? ['peaceful planet']

Put your hand in front of your mouth and repeat the /P/ sound. Can you feel the puff of air?

Write the letter P on your whiteboard.

What other words beginning with the sound /P/ could we use to describe the planet?

Where does it say 'I'm coming to get you!' on this page? How many words are there in that phrase?

Which word says 'you'?

Can we read the phrase and when we get to the word 'you' make it sound like a monster howling?

Which letters in the word 'you' make the /OO/ sound?

Work with a partner. Share a whiteboard. Write some more words that have the /OO/ sound. Share your favourite with another pair of children.

One of our theories behind this kind of exchange is that phonics teaching which is imbedded in children's understanding of interesting texts is more likely to be successful than phonics teaching which is decontextualised. Even psychological research that is critical of the statistical gains made by whole-language teaching has conceded that use of real texts to contextualise reading teaching is essential.

Texts

The essence of creativity in reading begins with the opportunity to discover your own texts to get excited about. There are times when reading is an enjoyable, emotional, stimulating, thought-provoking, escapist, therapeutic (and many other things that are personal to the reader) experience that has no need for analysis. At other times personal responses (including analysis and critique) are articulated with explicit in-depth knowledge of the text being read and the ability to compare with other texts. Getting excited about texts is not just for children; teachers and lecturers need this as well. So, in this spirit here are a few other texts that have interested us recently.

Dominic was reading *Exploring Children's Literature* (Gamble and Yates 2002) when he came across a reference to what sounded like an interesting book called *The Mysteries of Harris Burdick* (Van Allsburg 1984). The pictures in the book are like black-and-white photographs and have the kind of mesmeric, quiet, slightly unnerving atmosphere that is characteristic of some of Maurice Zendak's work. The story of the book is created by a convincing riddle. Harris Burdick wandered into a publisher's with a series of pictures with captions. He said that each picture came from a full story and that he would return with the stories, but he never did. The publisher was amazed by the pictures but was never able to find Burdick again. The pictures in the book, and the riddle, provide a classic stimulus for creative writing activities: what kind of stories would children write in response to the pictures?

The idea of playfulness in terms of writing and creativity is a very important one and it is something that also features in *The Adventures of Super Diaper Baby* (Beard and Hutchins 2002). The book is a graphic story which, internationally, is an important form but one which is often neglected in English schools. The first section explains how the writers were in trouble at school so they were made to do some writing as a punishment. But they were not allowed to write the story of *Captain Underpants* again, so they came up with *Super Diaper Baby*. The language is packed with jokes and games. Apart from the deliberately self-aware opening there are also other genre tricks. There are information sections which tell you how to draw the main characters and explanations about how to enjoy 'flip-o-rama' (flicker-book images), which is an ingenious way of introducing moving images in a printed text. There are also some intriguing asides to the reader:

> You know, since nobody reads these pages, we figured they'd be a good place to insert subliminal messages: Think for yourself. Question Authority. Read banned books! Kids have the same constitutional rights as grown-ups!!! Don't forget to boycott standardized testing!!!
>
> (Beard and Hutchins 2002: 76)

The book is written colloquially and includes the kinds of spelling and grammatical originality that a child writer might use: 'Our story Begins as a caR is speding to the Hospital. Hurry up! I'm Hurry Upping!' (*ibid.*)

Apart from telling you about a couple of books that we happen to be interested in, you can see that we have created a personal and, to some extent, analytic response to the books. This can be taken a little further. Although Gamble and Yates (2002) made us aware of *Harris Burdick*, we might argue with their claim that these represent 'unconventional' narrative structures. We also dispute the wide range of claims that narratives and other texts follow predictable genre structures. This is almost like saying that star signs really do predict our lives! It is true that there are commonly recognisable characteristics to particular kinds of texts but these are in some ways the least important aspect. It seems to us that playfulness, and hence originality, in texts is central, not peripheral, to the essence of the best children's literature. The importance of the ways that previous texts influence new texts; texts which discover new ways of directly connecting with children's lives; the importance of images; and our questioning of the snobbery of some children's literature analysis are also all themes which inform our personal response to texts, and, as we have already suggested, it is the personal creative response to texts that is important and that has been neglected in schools in recent years.

The quality of the texts that are available for children to read in the school and the classroom is at the heart of creative reading. This requires knowledgeable co-ordinators and teachers who can make expert selections for the children. Once the texts are chosen then children need to be able to make choices about which ones they read. This will help them develop and articulate their personal preferences. Teachers need to encourage discussion about texts: Which text have you chosen to read? Do you like it? Why? What did you think about the text that you have just finished? You say that but can you give me an example from the text? Do you know any other books by that author? Are there any similarities/ differences? We've all read *Skellig*; what kind of ideas do you remember from the text? These kinds of discussions can be followed by a wide range of activities inspired by texts. However, there is much to be gained from simply choosing, reading, thinking and talking.

Writing

If reading is like music performance then writing is like music composition. The composition of writing usually requires considerable amounts of creativity although this is not the case in the context of writing skills activities such as verb-spotting. The creativity that should be part of composition is also reduced if all children are set the same task by the teacher. Task-setting removes the children's opportunity to create their own purposes, decide their audience and create their own forms of writing. However, the setting of a writing task does allow some creativity in terms of the words to choose and minor layout features. You might assume that the teaching of writing has always been dominated by objective-led activities with little room for creativity. This is not the case and it is interesting to look back to the 1960s and 1970s when the creative writing movement was at its height.

Creative writing came about as a reaction to earlier rather formal approaches to the teaching of writing and English. One of the most influential texts from this time was Alec Clegg's book *The Excitement of Writing*. Clegg recognised the extensive use – and potentially damaging effect – of published English schemes and wanted to show examples in his book of children's writing 'taken from schools which are deliberately encouraging each child to draw sensitively on his own store of words and to delight in setting down his own ideas in a way which is personal to him and stimulating to those who read what he has written' (Clegg 1964: 4).

The creative writing approach involved the teacher providing a stimulus, such as a piece of music or visual art, which was followed by an immediate response. This often resulted in brief personal forms of writing such as a short descriptive sketch or a poem. The positive features of this were the emphasis on creativity and an early attempt to link writing with the arts. However, one of the problems was the fact that all the children still had to complete the teacher-designed task. The use of a stimulus for a group is often very successful but children need to find the kinds of stimuli that personally motivate them to write. Just like children, professional writers find their inspiration in different ways. As an example, here is what Philip Pullman, the author of the *His Dark Materials* trilogy, reveals about stimulus:

> I did *Paradise Lost* at 'A' level, and it's stayed with me all the way through until I was beginning to think about *Northern Lights* [the first book of the trilogy]. But my writing of the book came as a result of a meeting with David Fickling of Scholastic Books. David said he wanted me to do a book for him. I said that what I really wanted to do was *Paradise Lost* for teenagers. So he asked me to develop the idea. Off the top of my head I improvised a kind of fantasia on themes from Book 2 of *Paradise Lost* . . . By this time I knew the kind of thing I wanted to do – I knew the length, I knew it was going to be in three volumes and I knew it was going to be big and ambitious and enable me to say things I'd never been able to say in any other form.
>
> (Carter 1999: 188)

Notice here the way another text was the inspiration; the social aspect of being a writer shown through the conversation with a publisher which was also a stimulus; the importance of knowing how long a piece of writing is going to be; and the opportunity to say what you want (within the limits of libel laws). Other writers approach things in different ways; for example, Helen Cresswell treats writing as a long road and doesn't know where it is going until she gets there.

Protherough (1978) provided a very useful summary of the impact of creative writing and his paper also signalled some of the criticisms that were emerging. Overall he felt that the creative writing movement was an important one and that 'the emphasis on personal, imaginative writing [needed] to be maintained and extended' (p.18). But he felt the model had some weaknesses. One of these weaknesses was the restriction on the forms of writing that were used. The model did not encourage the writing of other forms such as argument, plays, or even short stories. Protherough (*ibid.*) recommended that 'the stimulated writing is to be seen *not* as the end-product, but as a stage in a process. Pupils need to be helped to develop their work, and to learn from each other as well as from the teacher.' In view of these kinds of criticisms, the use of artistic stimuli to produce creative writing is now used more selectively and to better effect. There is recognition that its techniques do indeed help with the development of personal creative responses and more imaginative use of language, but it is recognised that other forms of writing require different kinds of stimuli.

Here is an example of a teacher working with a Year 4 class who are used to cross-curricular creative writing. On one occasion children had been working with acrylic paint and looking at ways in which they could create moods and feelings using a limited palette of two colours (see Figure 1.1). Acrylic paint had been used on sheets of watercolour paper in a completely abstract manner, allowing different strokes and hues to meet, as though the surface was a sketchbook of ideas about the ways in which these colours could meet.

A week later these sheets were brought out for another art lesson. The teacher asked each child to select areas of interest from the sheet; areas where the strokes and/or the colour seemed to convey movement or a mood. Pupils were asked to rip out these areas (rather than cut them) and not to worry about the resulting bared white edges. Pupils were then asked to arrange these newly isolated areas into a collage. The teacher was keen to point out that the resulting image did not have to represent anything other than the mood suggested by the individual pieces. Pupils were encouraged to look at reassembling the pieces in ways which would deliberately contradict the original design in order to create a completely different surface.

An extended writing session began with these newly constructed 'mood collages'. Some pupils had built up from the surface of the paper and allowed the collage to take on other dimensions, but most of the results were two-dimensional. The white, ripped parts had been incorporated so that they looked like clouds, or like a landscape. The teacher asked each pupil to draft a written 'mood'

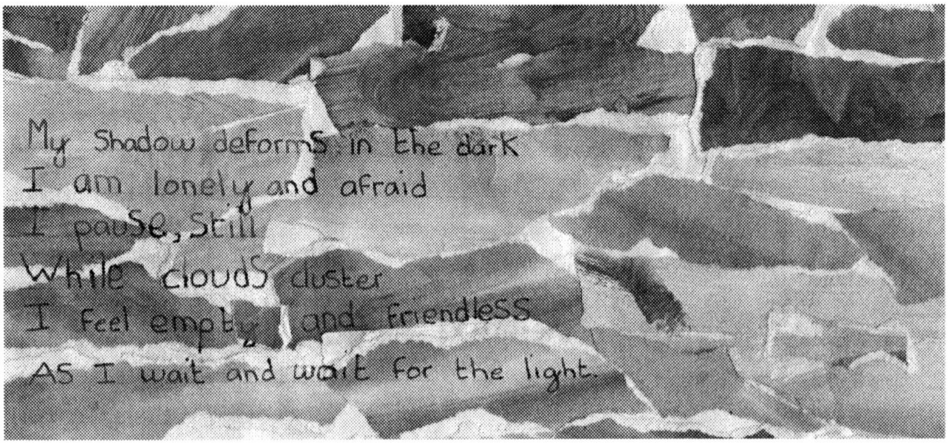

My Shadow deforms in the dark
I am lonely and afraid
I pause, still
While clouds cluster
I feel empty and friendless
As I wait and wait for the light.

Figure 1.1

response: to construct a four- or six-line response to the image, allowing the two to work together to 'explain' what kind of emotional response was being portrayed. Again, the teacher was keen to encourage responses which were not about 'how I feel right now . . .', but more along the lines of writing 'in character', about generating a written account of the mood represented by each collage.

The importance of poetic writing was a driving force for the teacher and the use of ripped-up texts a very useful strategy for developing poetic and creative language.

Russell: Why did you set up this process? Is it something you've done before?

Teacher: Actually, I've never done that before, but I'm pleased with the results. To be honest, it is something I hadn't planned to do at the start of the term but it came out of the work we have been doing on colour. Once I saw some of the experiments that had taken place I got really intrigued by the idea of where I could take this next. I've always liked the idea of ripping rather than cutting, and it seemed to be a natural progression.

Russell: The children seemed to understand what it was you wanted without much instruction. Why was that?

Teacher: Well I've been using rip-up techniques to teach poetry. You know how William Burroughs used to use that whole 'stream of consciousness' approach to writing and then cut it up and reassemble it to create 'new' ways of telling – well I kind of adapted that for my class. We tend to use that as a starting point – children fill up as many pages as they like with initial ideas and then the ripping and reassembling process means that you end up with really interesting combinations of words; words that were never intended to be next to each other suddenly seem to belong to each other, or then set off new trains of thought. We've done this for a while now and they are quite comfortable with it. It's a kind of route into poetry writing, I think, for those who feel that poetry isn't for them or that it's just limericks.

Russell: Well I saw some children shuffling their words around on their desks and playing with them . . .

Teacher: That's what they were doing. Some have moved on from that now and feel more confident about putting ideas on paper, however tentative they may be. The point is that I wanted them to see this as a starting process; it's not just assemblage, it's a starting point, the words should set off a larger process of writing.

Russell: One of the things that really interested me was that they were all so different.

Teacher: Precisely. That's part of the reason I did it. It's too easy for children to all respond in an identical way to a given input from me, or for me to just shape what they do so that I end up with 30 versions of a poem I would have liked to have written. What we have today is a set of individual responses, to a high standard, and each one completed. I can't see the point of half-finished pieces of work; I think it's counter-productive in the classroom; it feels as though the children's responses aren't valued.

The process approach

Following the criticisms of the creative writing approach of the 1960s and 1970s, a new approach became very popular. The 'process approach' to writing offered a way for teachers to support children's individual writing needs with a high emphasis on creativity.

The process approach is delivered through writing workshops which take place at least once a week, but ideally more frequently. The workshop is a whole-class teaching session where all the children are encouraged to write. The motivation for this comes about mainly through the freedom of choice children are offered over their writing and also through the emphasis on real audiences for the writing. Classroom publishing routines (including bookmaking), which mirror professional ones, are established, with the children's completed texts becoming part of the class reading area. These texts are subject to all the typical interaction surrounding the professionally produced texts. The main audience for the children's books is their peers, although the teacher, family and friends, other children in the school, parents, other teachers and other school children are all potential audiences for the writers. Teaching takes place at the beginning of the session in the form of 'mini-lessons', in 'writing conferences' with individual children throughout, and whole-class sharing time at the end of, the session. (For a full exploration of the implications of the use of the process approach see Wyse (1998).)

A snapshot of the range of topics that a class of children were engaged in shows the diversity and creative ideas that result from the process approach:

Computer games and how to cheat
Two pupils came up with the idea. The teacher suggested a survey of other children in the school who might be able to offer ways of getting through the levels on computer games. The teacher also suggested a format which would serve as a framework for the writing about each game.

A book of patterns
Self-generated idea with the teacher offering guidance on the amount of text that would be required and the nature of that text.

Tools mania
A flair for practical design technology projects resulted in one of the pair of pupils choosing this topic which involved writing a manual for the use of tools. Both pupils found the necessary explanatory writing a challenge.

The new girl
The girl herself was new to the school and this story may have provided her with a means of exploring some of her own feelings when she first arrived.

Manchester United fanzine

This was a particularly welcome project as it involved three girls working on an interest they had in football. It was an opportunity to challenge the stereotypes connected with football. The teacher set a strict deadline as the project seemed to be growing too big and also suggested the girls send the finished magazine to the football club to see what they thought.

Football story

The pupil worked unaided only requesting the teacher's support to check transcription.

A book of children's games

Using a book from home, the pupil chose her favourite games and rewrote them in her own words.

Secret messages

Various secret messages were included in the book which the reader had to work out. This was aimed at the younger children and involved a series of descriptions of unknown objects which the reader had to find around the school.

Kitten for Nicole

This was an advanced piece of narrative; the teacher made minor suggestions for improving the ending. However, in the end, the child decided she didn't like the text and started on a new one without publishing this.

Book for young children

The two boys used pop-art style cartoons for the illustrations as a means of appealing to the younger children. The teacher gave some input on the kinds of material that were likely to appeal to the younger children. One of the pair tended to let the other do most of the work and the teacher encouraged the sharing out of tasks.

Football magazine

There had been an epidemic of football magazines and the teacher made a decision that this was to be the last one for a time in order to ensure a balance of forms. The two boys used ideas from various professional magazines combining photographs with their own text.

Information about trains

Great interest in one of the school's information books, which included impressive pull-out sections, was the stimulus for this text. At the time, the work in progress consisted of a large drawing of a train. The teacher had concerns that too much time spent on the drawing could become a strategy for avoiding writing.

The magic coat
An expertly presented dual language story which had been written with help from the child's mother for the Urdu script. The home computer had also been used to create borders and titles. The teacher's role simply involved taking an interest in the progress.

Catchphrase
Pupil's doodling had given the teacher an idea for an activity which involved devising catchphrases based on the television programme. This pupil decided to compile a book of her own catchphrases.

Chinwag
Originally, two pupils had been encouraged to devise and sell a school magazine. This included market research around the school, design, word-processing, editing other children's contributions, selling, accounting, etc. This was a large-scale project and the original editors felt they would like to delegate the responsibility for the second issue to someone else, so two new editors took over.

Newspaper
The idea came from the two pupils but coincided, fortuitously, with a competition organised by the local paper encouraging students to design their own paper. The children asked various people around the school to offer stories. Layout became an important issue. The children bought in their own camera and took pictures to illustrate their text. Computers were used to support layout.

Modern fairy tale
The two pupils were struggling for an idea so the teacher suggested they contact another school to find out the kinds of books that some of the pupils liked, with a view to writing one for them. The school was in a deprived area and had many more bilingual children than the two pupils were used to. They realised that their initial questionnaire would need modification if it was to be used again. The children at the other school expressed a preference for traditional stories so the two pupils decided to write a modern fairy tale. They were encouraged by the teacher to ask the opinion of bilingual peers on suitable subject matter and some information about India.

Joke book
The two pupils surveyed the children in the school for good jokes. This was a popular title and had been done before in the course of the year.

Knightrider

A book based on the favourite television programme of the pupil.

When children make real choices about their writing, including topic, form, who to collaborate with, the number of workshops to spend on the writing, layout, whether to publish or not, etc., they take inspiration from their interests and knowledge. It cannot be emphasised strongly enough how important this is for creativity and for motivation. It is also likely to result in better writing in general. Remember also the learning that takes place through publishing texts in the classroom. Primarily this gives the writing a meaningful purpose but it also allows for the generation of a range of writing skills that are firmly contextualised. Book-making is so valuable that it should be a standard activity in any classroom whether the process approach is used or not.

Assessing creatively

Another anecdote shows how we need not only to teach creatively but also to *assess* creatively. Dominic's daughter Esther was preparing for her KS1 SATs in 2001 and, unusually, her teacher encouraged the children to write a story of their choice. I say unusually because in the climate of objective-led lessons, modelling and scaffolding, children were very rarely able to write anything of their own choice, although it was ironic that this happened as part of preparation for the tests. The writing was sent home along with homework instructions which included the request to help correct any transcription errors. When Dominic and Esther's mum first saw the piece they were overjoyed to read the wonderful story. While discussing it with Esther it became clear that she was not keen on further redrafting because it was finished. Dominic suggested that he might work with Esther on the computer but this made no difference. In the end he typed up the piece in the hope that some comparison might be made between the transcription and the original. But Esther remained adamant that the piece was finished (the superscript font shows first attempts and crossings out):

THE TOTH FIRE [Decorated lettering]
One day a litt^{e}le girl lost 1 of her teeth. Her name was Cloe. Cloe was a good litel girl. Her tooth looked orenge.

'The nexst day Cloe and her^{mumy} mummy where having brecfest when the paper came. 'I will get it!' said Cloe. Mummy mummy! In the paper it said there is a very^f bad FIRE! Well come her and I will tell you a story. When I was a litt^{e}le girl and there was a fire. And I had just lost a tooth and^{tat} that was orenge. And I said to my mum can I thro my tooth away Wy don't you thro it in the fire. So I said OK. And can you ges wat hapend the fire whent out. Shal I do that . . . if you wish. So she whent to find the fire. She thro the tooth into the fire and it aventhoole it went out.[1] Evrewon chead and shouted. WEL DONE CLOE. Then cloe ran home and toled her mumy. Mu^mmmy I put the fire out. Wel done nowe you no wat to do with yor tooth.

I began to think about the writing in relation to the test criteria which say that for level 3 writing:

> The writing communicates meaning in a way which is lively and generally holds the reader's interest.
>   Some characteristic features of a chosen form of narrative or non-narrative writing are beginning to be developed.

There were numerous things which I felt were lively and held my interest. The opening does this by beckoning the reader into the story: 'Well come her and I will tell you a story' – this was possibly influenced by a picture-book that Esther was familiar with called *The Dancing Frog*, which uses a similar technique. There were various aspects which represented characteristic features of narrative such as the use of dialogue, the moral to the story and the further explicit messages to the reader: 'and you can guess what happened'. The criteria also require that: 'Links between ideas or events are mainly clear and the use of some descriptive phrases adds detail or emphasis.' Examples such as 'good litel girl'; 'where having brecfest'; 'very bad FIRE!', in particular, the use of capitals and an exclamation mark, illustrated the description and detail. However, overall I felt that it was the spelling test which would bring the overall writing grade down to level 2. In the end this proved to be the case, in spite of level 3s for reading and maths.

The criteria for the statutory tests are only one rather limited, but worryingly influential, way to analyse children's writing, so I began to reflect on the comparison between the criteria and my own initial emotional response, wondering if my thoughts were just the effect of being a doting father. The writing had a cathartic element represented by the coming to terms with one of life's many rites of passage: losing a tooth. All writers generate ideas by explicitly and/or implicitly reflecting on their own lives. It contained a mystery to challenge the mind of the reader: could it be that only orange teeth would put out a fire? The best texts leave unresolved questions and food for thought. It gave personal messages to the reader which playfully disrupts fixed ideas about genre. Intertextuality is represented on a number of levels: the asides to the reader; the very bad fire in the newspaper; the potential influence of *The Dancing Frog*. The writing also mirrored some of the emotions to do with self-confidence which were a feature of Esther's life. Narrative has always offered a vehicle for exploring emotions.

But the most extraordinary revelation came only after I had discussed the *processes* that led to the draft. Esther was sat next to her friend and had only written a title for the piece. Her friend said: 'That's not how you spell "fairy", that says "fire". Rather than correct the spelling Esther constructed the complete narrative on the ideas of a tooth and a fire; like a metaphysical conceit perhaps. The creative dexterity and cognitive challenge of this is fascinating, but overall it reinforced my belief that the assessment of writing must take account of the process, not just the product. The whole episode also heightened my dissatisfaction with the criteria for the statutory tasks for English writing and led me to consider more important ones:

- How much *originality* is represented through *choice* and selection of ideas?
- How are real life and textual *influences* used?
- How much *thought* does the writing engender in readers?
- How *playful* is the writer?
- What kind of *emotional* response does the writing engender?
- What was the nature of thought during the *process* of writing.

These kinds of things can only be assessed through high-quality teacher assessment, which is one of the reasons that many people in education are calling for the replacement of statutory tests at age 7, 11 and 14 by more teacher assessment. As this looks unlikely to be the case, children's creativity may continue to suffer.

The creativity that is part of the subject of English is embedded in the texts that writers and readers engage with. We have shown examples of both creative teaching and creative learning and we have also pointed out that there are considerable barriers to creativity that can be overcome by skilful and confident teachers. In order to foster creativity in English further, the job of policy-makers should be to remove barriers, not keep adding more.

Creative touches

- Make a list of five things you would like to write about. Choose one of them and start writing!
- Tell your partner about your favourite book.
- Choose a character from your favourite book and take them for a walk. Let them visit a character from a different book and see how they get on!
- Help every child in your class write a book to go into the class reading area.
- Create a multimedia text that has words, pictures, animations and sounds.

- Ask two reluctant writers to set you a writing task. Ask them to decide the content and direction and let them watch you write for them! Now simply reverse the process.

- Make a list of the top ten books in the class.

- Be aware that teachers continually ask questions in the classroom. Ask children to list as many different *kinds* of questions asked in a day (how, why, what if… etc.). Try to go through a lesson without asking questions and instead offering comments, observations etc. and see how pupils respond differently.

- Cut some pictures out of the week's newspapers. Write the captions. Imagine the possible stories.

- Have an author of the week / book of the week / word of the week.

- Make a class joke book.

- Get a big box of poetry books. Browse through them. Find your favourite and perform it for the class with a friend.

- Split the class into groups of four or five. Ask them to choose a well known story, fairy tale, myth or legend. Let them decide on six tableaux; six still, posed images that will convey the whole story (see the work of John Airs). Take digital photos and import them into a word document where you can re-tell the story in the form of a new book. Read these to a younger class in another part of the school.

References
Beard, G. and Hutchins, H. (2002) *The Adventures of Super Diaper Baby*. London: Scholastic.

Carter, J. (1999) *Talking Books: Children's Authors Talk about the Craft, Creativity and Process of Writing*. London: Routledge.

Clegg, A. B. (1964) *The Excitement of Writing*. London: Chatto and Windus.

Coles, G. (2003) *Reading the Naked Truth: Literacy, Legislation, and Lies*. Portsmouth, NH: Heinemann.

Gamble, N. and Yates, S. (2002) *Exploring Children's Literature*. London: Paul Chapman.

Harrison, H. (2002) *Key Stage 3 English: Roots and Research*. London: Department for Education and Skills.

National Reading Panel (2001). *Home*. Retrieved 7 November 2003 from http://www.nationalreading-panel.org/

Protherough, R. (1978) 'When in doubt, write a poem'. *English in Education*, **12** (1): 9–21.

Tolkien, J. R. R. (1955) *The Lord of the Rings. Part Three: Return of the King*. Reprinted 2001. London: HarperCollins.

Van Allsburg, C. (1984) *The Mysteries of Harris Burdick*. Boston: Houghton Mifflin.

Wyse, D. (1998) *Primary Writing*. Buckingham: Open University Press.

CHAPTER 2

Mathematics

Una Hanley

'An over-emphasis on numeracy, literacy and testing in the core areas is stifling creativity' (BBC News, 24 June 2003) was typical of a number of news headlines at the time. Many people do not view mathematics as a natural home for creative thinking; Mathematics classrooms are deemed to be places where you get on with the serious business of teaching those skills that enable children to achieve the desired level in the national tests. Teaching to foster creativity happens elsewhere, if there is time.

It is easy to see why people do not associate creativity with mathematics. Mathematics is about rules, structure and following routines, isn't it? Rectangles have four right-angles, for example. Well, they do, but a recent trip to the Tate Modern was sufficient to remind anyone of the flair employed by Mondrian, Albers and Rothko (to name but a few) in adding a creative dimension to this familiar fact. These artists took shapes, particularly squares and arranged them to create a sense of colour and dimension in space.

In the area of mathematics, connecting creativity to cognition appears to be a useful place to begin. Cropley (2003) speculates that creativity might be described as taking the *structures* of thought (internal representations of the external world such as patterns, categories or networks); *processes* (e.g. exploring, organising, interpreting, applying); *control mechanisms* (e.g. decision-making – rules, evaluation strategies) and other things, the ability to challenge the customary 'hard-wiring' which we all normally employ to make sense of our experiences.

The ability to challenge conventional knowledge does not appear to be a key feature of modern primary classrooms. The experience in mathematics classrooms, for many of us, fosters an understanding of the subject which privileges the acquisition of facts and skills rather than stimulates the imagination. For many, the seat for imagination is problem-solving. Problem-solving has been recognised as an important part of mathematics for a long time: 'The ability to solve problems is at the heart of mathematics' (Department of Education and Science/The Welsh Office/Committee of Inquiry into the Teaching of Mathematics in Schools 1982: 69). This statement clarifies the purpose of the mathematics curriculum. Therefore, we should learn skills in order to be able to use them; but this is not the entire story. Problem-solving requires us to make decisions about which skills to use; to adapt, extend and develop those we have; to use them thoughtfully and ingeniously and to experience enjoyment and satisfaction in the process. Problem-solving is a process which is intrinsic to creativity (Cropley 2003).

One definition of problem-solving is mathematics applied to situations and contexts which in other respects may not be particularly mathematical. These are frequently described as 'real life problems' or problems drawn from the whole curriculum. Other definitions of problem-solving suggest exploring within mathematics itself: puzzles, games and investigative mathematics. A third definition sees mathematics as 'practical tasks' (Billington *et al.* 1991: 5).

In 1988 the Non-Statutory Guidance which accompanied the National Curriculum document for maths (National Curriculum Council 1988: 8–9) clarified these recommendations. For example, in the section about schemes of work, the following recommendations are made:

5.1 Activities should bring together different areas of mathematics.
5.3 The order of activities should be flexible and pupils should be involved in determining their own next targets.
5.7 Activities should, where appropriate, use pupils' own interests or questions either as starting points or as further lines of development.
5.8 Activities should, where appropriate, involve both independent and co-operative work.
5.10 Activities should be balanced between different modes of learning: doing, observing, talking and listening, discussing with other pupils, reflecting, drafting, reading and writing etc.

Using and applying mathematics in the 2000 National Curriculum, which is now seen as a crucial part of all maths attainment targets, offers a flavour of the original intentions. Pupils should be taught to solve problems, learn to communicate mathematically and develop the powers to reason and to think logically. However, the document focuses on the outcomes for pupils rather than the strategies and approaches to the curriculum that teachers need to consider. This kind of information is found in the National Numeracy Strategy (NNS) which was written to tackle perceived low standards in calculation which is where its focus lies (hence the title *numeracy*). References to problem-solving tend to centre on 'sums with words' rather than on a more creative and reflective *process*.

Some people argue that the National Numeracy Strategy has been successful, as children's ability to calculate appears to have improved and many teachers feel that the documentation has been very helpful in enabling them to see how mathematical skills can be developed over time. But the focus on facts and skills – the kind of mathematics associated with calculation – has meant that other aspects have been neglected.

Those in doubt that the world of mathematics is both a creative one and one where problem-solving is central should read Simon Singh's (1997) account of how Andrew Wiles solved a mathematical riddle that had taxed the greatest mathematicians for more than 300 years. Wiles said: 'Since the age of ten, I have been hooked on mathematical problems as intellectual challenges' (Department for Education and Employment (DfEE) and the Qualifications and Curriculum Authority (QCA) 1999: 61).

Not everyone will want to be a professor of mathematics, but at all levels mathematics teaching should foster individual curiosity, challenge and the opportunity to be creative. The writers of the Cockcroft Report (and other mathematics educators) view problem-solving as essential to this aim, recommending mathematical activities which offer children the opportunity to practise the skills they know, to reason, interpret and communicate in a variety of ways in familiar and unfamiliar contexts.

Teaching and learning

When I asked a number of colleagues and teachers of mathematics across the age phases what they thought creativity in mathematics might mean there were a number of surprising replies, including remarks like 'What's that?' Other responses included:

- Many teachers prefer literacy to mathematics. In mathematics, teachers are rarely confident enough to work outside the documents.
- The format of the Numeracy Hour and the focus on lesson objectives means that it's difficult to challenge this way of doing things.
- All the coloured resources in the world don't make for a creative lesson unless the children are asked to work with them in a way that extends their thinking.
- You can't be creative if you don't have some skills in the first place. Every artist needs to learn how to hold their tools, but you need freedom to use them. This is the case for both teachers and pupils.
- Creativity isn't something you just 'throw' into the mathematics curriculum and expect it to flourish. Other things have to be in place already. The children have to be used to sharing tasks, talking to one another and being creative in other areas. There needs to be a general ethos in the classroom (and in the school) which values children's interests and opinions.

- Being creative is about finding ways of extending what you know in other areas like art or history. Teachers need to see the opportunities for mathematics outside mathematics lessons.

- Sometimes I think it's the teachers who have to learn to be creative. Some teaching styles in maths classrooms are very didactic and don't make space for children's thinking. If the teacher thinks maths is about routines, then lessons will be boring.

- Children can't be creative if they are not given the chance to decide what to do for themselves. You have to set them a task in which there's lots of space for them to decide what to do using the knowledge they have.

- The danger of any new initiative is that eventually, in a busy classroom, it becomes another thing to tick in a box. If we are 'ordered' to be creative the same thing will happen, if it's just added to what we do.

Beliefs and approaches to mathematics are very important. If the teacher thinks of mathematics as a set of skills to practise, and rules to learn, then this is what they will focus on in their teaching. Anything else tends to be seen as 'in addition to' and there may never be time to do it. Creativity cannot only be a one-off activity. It should be a characteristic of an approach to the curriculum which values every child's interests and styles of learning and encourages them to use their skills in new contexts. Existing tight lesson formats with specific objectives do not lend themselves to approaches which value children's interests.

We all remember the teachers that we liked and admired. While mathematics was not the favoured subject for many, people do tend to remember maths teachers who didn't just stand at the front of the class, but found ways to make topics interesting or who gave their pupils stimulating things to do. In *Effective Teachers of Numeracy* (Askew *et al.* 1997: 31–2) the authors connect knowledge of the subject, knowledge of how pupils learn mathematics, and knowledge of teaching approaches into three different orientations towards mathematics teaching. These are described as *connectionist, transmission* and *discovery*. Here is a short extract from the report to give you a flavour of the kinds of issues being addressed:

Connectionist teachers believe:
- Learning about mathematical concepts and the ability to apply these concepts are learned together.
- The connections between mathematical ideas needs to be acknowledged in teaching.
- Application is best approached through challenges that need to be reasoned about.
- Teaching is based on dialogue.

Transmission teachers believe:

- Learning about mathematical concepts precedes the ability to apply these concepts.
- Mathematical ideas need to be introduced in discrete packages.
- Application is best approached through 'word' problems: contexts for calculating routines.
- Teaching is based on verbal explanations.

Discovery teachers believe:

- Learning about mathematical concepts precedes the ability to apply these concepts.
- Mathematical ideas need to be introduced in discrete packages.
- Application is best approached through using practical equipment.
- Teaching is based on practical activities.

Although teachers exhibitit characteristics from more than one orientation, those with a strong connectionist view are most frequently described as effective. Here, effectiveness refers to the ability of teachers to support children in making sense of mathematical structure as opposed to the more usual reference to 'neatly packaged' lesson objectives and curriculum management. These teachers are not necessarily deemed to be those with the best qualifications on paper, e.g. those with a first degree in maths (Brown *et al.* 1999). Overall, the authors suggest that teachers with a connectionist orientation adopt the most appropriate approaches to teaching and these approaches support interpersonal activity, challenge, reasoning and an understanding 'of the links between different aspects of the mathematics curriculum' (*ibid.*: 31). This kind of teacher is also likely to foster creativity.

We now turn to a couple of examples of such teachers at work. While the use of calculators in the classroom continues to be the subject of debate, the Calculator Aware Number curriculum (CAN) project showed clearly that calculators can be used to stimulate the imagination of children and encourage them to experiment with numbers. The calculator supports children's thinking in areas of number and number operations which are beyond their fluency in calculating skills. Although the CAN project was discontinued some years ago, their materials are still in school and continue to be used by teachers.

Case study 1: extending existing lesson plans in numeracy

Mrs Newton's Year 3 classroom was a busy place. She was an experienced teacher and told everyone, including the children, that she enjoyed teaching mathematics. She felt that while an emphasis on mental calculation was important, teachers had become afraid to use calculators in case children came to rely on them too much. However, in her view calculators offered many opportunities for children to 'think for themselves' as they supported their work with larger numbers. The children had worked with calculators before, chiefly in activities which promoted the practice of multiplication. On this occasion Mrs Newton had a slightly different task: she explained to the children that she had chosen 13 as it was an odd number and supposed to be unlucky.

Task: 'If thirteen is the answer, what's the question?'

There was no written plan for the lesson. Mrs Newton had no particular objectives in mind other than to offer children the opportunity to work on a different style of task which was sufficiently open-ended to allow them to 'take risks'. She felt that her experience and confidence would enable her to work profitably on the different solutions that the children offered.

There was a general hubbub as children began to discuss the task and started to write down some suggestions. Answers were quickly forthcoming, many of which had clearly not been dependent upon the calculator.

$$6 + 7 = 13$$
$$10 + 3 = 13$$
$$8 + 5 = 13$$

All the addition complements to 13 were quickly found and put in order. 'Are there any other questions you can ask where thirteen is the answer?' asked Mrs Newton. Children began to talk to one another. This was clearly a bit of a sticking point. '14 – 1 = 13', someone suggested eventually. Mrs Newton wrote this on the board and a buzz of activity followed.

Michael was frequently obliged to work on his own as Mrs Newton felt that he had difficulty maintaining attention and disrupted some of the other children. He covered his work with his arm when she approached. Mrs Newton commented on someone else's suggestion:

Seventeen minus four – good!
Twenty minus seven – good!

Lots more suggestions followed: 'I hope you are writing these down!' The list got longer and Mrs Newton asked them to put their suggestions in order. What could they see? 'When you add, all the numbers in one column come down and go up in the other.'

12 + 1	20 – 7
11 + 2	19 – 6
10 + 3	18 – 5

This was clearly familiar territory. 'Have you got to get them all?' someone asked. 'How will we know if we have them all?' asked Mrs Newton. Some of the children abandoned the calculator and began to 'fill in' the columns. The children worked away at this for several minutes. In the meantime, Michael had been unusually quiet. Mrs Newton approached and insisted on seeing his efforts. Michael had written $10 + 3 = 13$ and several other examples of addition complements which he had not put in order. Then:

$17 - 4 = 13$

$20 - 7 = 13$

$21 - 8 = 13$

$23 - 10 = 13$

$30 - 17 = 13$

$40 - 27 = 13$

$50 - 37 = 13$ (and so on . . .)

$90 - 77 = 13$

$100 - 87 = 13$

$200 - 187 = 13$

$300 - 287 = 13$ (and so on . . .)

$800 - 787 = 13$

$900 - 887 = 13$

$1000 - 987 = 13$ . . . [and from here he got a little stuck]

$10000 - 9870 = 13$

$100000 - 98700 = 13$

Michael, in full flow, had abandoned the calculator. Mrs Newton was astounded. Clearly the task had engaged Michael and he was able to experiment with numbers in a creative way. Although Michael's work was impressive, other children also had extended pieces of work. Sharing solutions encouraged those who had worked slowly and safely to take more risks.

Why is this offered as an example of creativity in the curriculum?

- The activity was accessible and open-ended.
- There was space for children to experiment with and extend established understanding. There was the possibility of awakening new thoughts and ideas.
- It stimulated discussion and raised questions as to how things might be recorded.
- The activity was very motivating and enjoyable.
- From the teacher's perspective, it was not difficult to arrange and did not require any special resources other than a calculator.

Case study 2: a 'real life' problem

Problem-solving has been an important feature of the mathematics curriculum for a number of years, particularly with the introduction of the National Curriculum. Unfortunately, there is some confusion about the nature of problem-solving. Some teachers still equate problem-solving with solving word problems. For example:

> Tins of beans cost 27p at the supermarket. Oranges are 21p each. If I buy two tins of beans and three oranges, how much have I spent?

These kinds of calculations, contextualised in familiar settings, are understood to be examples of problem-solving for many teachers. The tasks certainly set problems. Children find 'sums with words' difficult to read and difficult to translate into a form which lends itself to the kinds of calculations with which they are familiar. 'I don't know what to do' is a common enough cry for help. Solving 'real life' problems, however, gives children the opportunity to bring the 'world outside' into the classroom and, in so doing, makes opportunities for children to use their developing skills in meaningful as well as creative and purposeful ways.

With these ideas in mind Miss Collins had asked a group in her Year 2 class to plan a party. She felt that she needed to work harder to 'bridge the gap' between the mathematics taught in maths lessons and the kinds of challenges in life outside the classroom where mathematical skills might be useful. In thinking about this, Miss Collins hoped to make cross-curricular links, something she felt happened too infrequently. During the 1970s, 1980s and early 1990s the primary curriculum was planned by teachers through the use of 'topics' with the explicit goal of making strong cross-curricular links. However, in the 1990s a number of criticisms were levelled at topic work, particularly in relation to mathematics. Most topics did not include mathematics, or if they did, it was frequently in trivial ways. For example, a topic about the seaside might acknowledge the presence of mathematics by requiring children to use shells as counting resources. Topics were rarely constructed around mathematics. It was Miss Collins' intention to do just this.

Task: plan a party for the class

The children approached the task with their existing skills but had to find ways of applying what they knew creatively to new contexts. Many of the associated tasks were open-ended insofar as children sought to find the 'best' among a number of possible outcomes. Importantly, something was going to happen as a consequence, for which they were responsible.

The teacher was able to foresee some difficulties. Children were unaccustomed to working in this way and would need a lot of help and support. They would need to use their judgement as well as their skills, and they would probably need considerable encouragement. Additionally, the children taking part would have to learn to work co-operatively for an extended period. For this reason, the task would not involve the whole class in the first instance.

Miss Collins' lesson plans were not directly related to National Curriculum or Numeracy Strategy objectives, but this was obviously possible. In many ways, decisions were made *in situ* and discussed afterwards. Miss Collins was aware of the questions and problems likely to arise and how she might encourage children to take the initiative.

Lesson 1

Aims: To introduce the problem at hand and to begin to use past knowledge to plan what they will need.

Possible activities: Children to brainstorm ideas and to create a list of items which would be needed for the party.

Children tended to suggest their own favourites:

Stephen had a very extensive list including cultural foods and personal preferences such as rice, turkey, stuffing. Other ideas included having fish and chips or getting 'Happy Meals' from McDonald's. Although the ideas were imaginative, I chose to ask the group if such items were OK for a school party. The group also reached a disagreement when it came to the drinks we would need.

The conversation went as follows:

Jason: We could have orange juice for the children and tea for the teachers.
Fiona: I don't like orange juice, I like Vimto.
Daniel: I don't like Vimto!
Sharon: Oh no! Everyone likes different drinks, we can't buy them all!
Jason: That would be too much money.
Teacher: Why don't we buy the drink that people like the best, the most favourite drink?
Michelle: Yeah, we will have to ask everyone in the class what drink they like best.
Fiona: Okay, but we'll have to have Vimto 'cos that's what I want.
(At this point, Miss Collins asked them to make a list for sandwich fillings.)
Sharon: Don't forget the bread and butter!

Miss Collins also found it difficult to leave the problem to the children. She felt that the question of how the flavour of the drinks might be decided needed a firm hand. Other impractical and inappropriate ideas were raised. However, the children could see the problems they had created for themselves and did come up with alternative ideas. It was clear to them that everyone's opinion needed to be canvassed.

Lesson 2

Aims: To encourage children to use different methods of data collection and discuss fair practice and appropriate research.

   Possible activities:

- Recap on what the children suggested last week and discuss how decisions will be made in relation to purchases.
- Encourage children to collect data.
- Assemble a final shopping list and cost it out.

The lesson began with a review of what had been done previously. All of the children were very enthusiastic about their own task and immediately gathered scrap paper and went to ask the other children in the class for their preferences, all except Daniel. He sat at the desk and wrote all the different types of drinks he could think of. After observing everyone else in the group he then asked if he had to write everyone's name, or whether he could just put ticks next to the drinks. This was a different approach from the others. Other children wrote everyone's name and the response next to it. Some children left their paper on the table and went to ask each child for their preference before returning to ask for spellings and to write it down. Some children also needed help checking their results which made it hard for the teacher to maintain the role of facilitator. Children found it difficult to wait for their turn, to think up their own methods for collecting data or to apply those they had been taught. They had to be prompted. Miss Collins had hoped that more of the children might have adopted Daniel's approach, using their past knowledge. However, children had been given the opportunity to discuss their methods and findings and to decide which methods had been the most suitable. They all liked Daniel's method – ticks rather than lists of children's names (see Figure 2.1).

Lesson 3

Aim: Children to find out how much individual items cost as preparation for costing the party.

   Possible activity: A visit to Aldi to price food to discuss the problems posed by multipacks

   It took patience and careful organisation to arrange a visit to the local supermarket. The 'table' of purchases that the children were to use as a basis for the shopping was teacher-designed, although everyone completed the table from the lists which had been compiled (see Table 2.1).

   This was done in order to save time and to sustain the children's interest. Once in the supermarket the children were very enthusiastic, even adding items such as napkins and plates to the lists.

Choclact √√√√ 4
CarmLe √√√ 3
Custard crEm √√√√√√√√√√ 4
anmul biscvits √√√√√ 4
Cvmis √√ 2
10 ☆
 Tam √√√
gingn √√√√√

10

Figure 2.1 Daniel's tick lists

They only had a few minor problems in recording their findings. One thing that confused the children was the fact that both the ice-cream and orange juice came in litres. The teacher said, 'I saw this as a teaching opportunity and I began to explain that a litre is an amount of liquid, but I decided to go over this again next session in the classroom'.

Jason started to work out how many of each packet of food would be needed. He said that if the cakes came in packs of five, and there are 16 children altogether coming to the party, then five and five and five and five would be needed, which makes 20, which he demonstrated using his fingers. Michelle suggested that that was too many cakes, to which Jason replied, 'Yes, but five and five and five is fifteen and that's not enough'. It was agreed that too many was

Table 2.1

Our class shopping list

Item for the party	How much does it cost?	How many do you get?
Loaf of Bread	19P	1
Carton of butter	35P	1
Jelly	17P	1
Ice-cream	99P	1 liter
chees and onion	49P	6
tuna	29P	1
orange juice	29P	1 liter
custar cream	45P	32
chocolate cakes	79P	5
cherryade	89P	6
ham	£1,79P	1
crakes	69P	1
jam	59P	1
MiLk	49P	1
Plaper Plates	99p	8
napkins	99p	20

better than too few. It was rewarding to find a context in which counting up in fives had a real purpose.

It was clear that as the task progressed the children were beginning to grasp that the party posed quite a complex problem. They recognised that the big problem was made up of lots of smaller ones and they were beginning to redefine the problems and refine the work as they went along. Miss Collins also felt that she had a much clearer idea of the understanding that children had in a number of areas of the curriculum, particularly numeracy and data-handling.

Lesson 4

Aims: Use previous number skills and knowledge of base 10 to work out multiples of single- and two-digit numbers; count the money available, including pounds.

Possible activities:

- Count the 'biscuit money' which is being used to finance the party, calculating the number of multipacks required.
- Calculate the number of bottles of cordial required.

This was a difficult session. At first the children were reluctant to work out the number of multipacks they would require and needed a lot of prompting. Miss Collins began to feel a lot less like a facilitator. Eventually, the tasks were split among the children and they worked in pairs. Jason and Michelle were asked to work out how much drink they would need to buy.

Jason:	What does one litre mean, Miss?
Teacher:	A litre measures how much liquid there is. In this bottle there is one litre of juice. How can we work out how much we need?
Jason:	We could see how many drinks you get from one bottle.
Michelle:	But you can't drink it like that! You have to put water in it with a cup.
Teacher:	Well it says here when you dilute it, when you add water to it, you add four parts water to one part juice [pointing to the label on the bottle].
Michelle:	That means that if you have a litre of juice you add four litres of water. That makes [thinking] five litres!
Jason:	Really?
Michelle:	Yeah! One add four . . . five!
Teacher:	Okay, but how are we going to find out how many we need to buy?
Michelle:	We can add juice to four litres of water and pour it into cups [there were some cups in the classroom by the sink]. We will need 16 cups-full.
Teacher:	OK, well here I have a measuring jug that holds one litre so you can use this.

The two children then went on to use a large jug and filled it up using litres of water from the measuring jug. Jason counted how many litres they had used and Michelle counted the cups while they took turns to pour the water out. They placed 16 cups out and filled them all. Other pairs also worked on this task.

Figure 2.2 Michelle's party suggestions

Some children used 'multilink' to model the multipacks, a choice that some of them made of their own accord, although they had to be helped to find the total cost of a number of packs. Miss Collins suggested that it might be useful to use the computer so that their work would look more presentable. This was agreed with enthusiasm. The teacher said 'This helped me to see if the children could generalise their ideas in graphical as well as oral form, for others to view'.

Lesson 5

This lesson focused on data-handling and the use of the school's data-handling software. A wall display was planned and the children discussed the questions they might ask of one another; for example, 'How many children like fairy cakes?' 'What is the most popular flavour of crisps, and what is the second most popular?'

Lesson 6

This was the day of the party. Miss Collins had been shopping for the food, feeling that another trip to the supermarket was not only difficult to arrange but also unnecessary as all the calculating had been done. It was enjoyed hugely.

The children had remained motivated and involved, even though some of the preparation for the party had created some difficult calculations. Miss Collins felt that this was because the tasks were not seen as 'school mathematics', and were much more purposeful. The children had employed the strategies they knew and extended them. Miss Collins had tried to resist 'stepping in' and children had frequently seen the need to do things differently, as in the case of finding out the most popular drinks. There were lots of 'oh yeah!' moments. The task had also provided a purpose for the use of the data-handling package which the children thought did justice to their efforts.

Miss Collins had found the P.R.O.B.L.E.M.S. acronym useful in selecting her task:

Pose the problem – What is the problem? What can we do about it? (This works well as a brainstorming session where all ideas are valued and written down.)

Redefining into areas for investigation – decide what the problem is and what needs investigating (usually worked on by children dividing up into groups).

Outline the questions to ask – What do we need to find out? Will we be able to answer the questions? Will the answers help us solve the problem?

Bring the data home – collect the information needed.

Look for solutions – Can we find a clear result? Did the information answer our questions?

Establish recommendations – How will solutions/outcomes fit together?

Make it happen.

So what now?

She knew that there were a number of other descriptions of problem-solving but felt that this had been particularly accessible. She felt that the task had enabled her to offer children the opportunities to work at each of the criteria suggested by the acronym.

Why is this study offered as an example of creativity in the curriculum? The children had been encouraged to look at their mathematics differently. The children were honing their mathematical skills – calculation and data-handling – but within a context which gave these purpose. In this problem there were opportunities to make choices, but these had to be explained and justified to others. Importantly, children had to be encouraged to overcome difficulties. Most significantly, the children had had to make a number of important decisions for themselves and then work with those decisions. The day of the party marked a proud moment.

The case studies illustrate class teachers who are teaching mathematics creatively. The first study depicted a teacher working on an activity which she found easy to integrate with the planned curriculum which is a very useful place to begin, if you are trying these kinds of ideas for the first time. The other case study showed an extended number of lessons devoted to particular tasks. This kind of teaching and learning takes much more organisation and requires the teacher to be committed to the interest and learning they generate.

As a teacher it is difficult not to be overwhelmed by the demands of delivering the curriculum. But you should remember that teaching and learning is much more than simple 'delivery'. In many ways, delivery is a very unfortunate term as the emphasis is on a 'product' being completed rather than something which builds on the views of those who are the 'consumers'. Learners have views and perspectives, preferences and strengths which need to be considered. If the mathematics on offer does not extend their imaginations in a number of ways, including their ability to calculate, they will come to see mathematics as the subject where the chief pleasure, if there is one, lies in getting their sums right.

Creative touches

- Sum-u-like. Turn a hard sum that you are working on into an easier one that you like. For example:

  35×21

  21 can be read as $(2 \times 10) + 1$, so the calculation becomes:

  $35 \times (2 \times 10 + 1)$

  $35 \times 2 = 70$

  $70 \times 10 = 700$

  $700 + (1 \times 35) = 735$

The issue is to encourage children to want to apply strategies that have perhaps been taught because they can see that it's a useful thing to be able to do.

● Using the numbers 2 0 0 3 (or any other year) and any operation, make all the numbers between 0 and 50.

1 would be made by using 3 − 2

7 would be made by 2 × 2 plus 3

Start with a year where the digits are 'friendly', e.g. 1953. Decide if you have to use all the digits in each calculation or only some of them. Decide if you can use any digit more than once in each calculation. Decide if you are going to restrict the operations you use, and so on. Are there any numbers you can't make? If so, why?

● Using the 3s and 5s rods from 'Colour Factor' make some number trains. For example, a train for 11 would be made up of 2 lots of '3' rods and a '5' rod. Which trains cannot be made?

● Make a class number book, e.g. 11 players, one team; 7 days, one week; 1 000 000 000, one sky of stars.

● Milk crate. A certain milk crate can hold 36 bottles of milk. Can you arrange 14 bottles in the crate so that each row and column has an even number of bottles?

● Make a square using four sticks. Add another square of sticks.

First example: 4 sticks; second example: 7 sticks; third example: 10 sticks. How many sticks in the ninth set of squares? . . . the 20th? . . . the 35th? How would you work out how many sticks you might need for the nth square? There are lots of pattern-spotting activities of this kind.

● This is the postcard the giant received (A1 size), draw his hand (foot, head, etc.).

● Make a life-line showing when you were born and the key events that have happened since then.

● On a 4 × 4 square: How many ways can the square be halved? Repeat your favourite 'half' to create a design. For example:

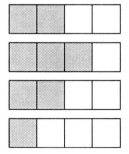

Try a 5 × 5 square.

- Tangram activities – a well-known 7-figure shape puzzle with endless possibilities.

References

Askew, M. *et al.* (1997) *Effective Teachers of Numeracy*. London: King's College.

Billington, J. *et al.* (1991) *Using and Applying Mathematics*. London: Association of Teachers of Mathematics.

Burton, L. (1994) *Children Learning Mathematics*. Hemel Hempstead: Simon and Schuster.

Cropley, A. J. (2003) *Creativity in Education and Learning: A Guide for Teachers and Educators*. London: Kogan Page.

Department for Education and Employment (DfEE) and the Qualifications and Curriculum Authority (QCA) (1999) *The National Curriculum: Handbook for Primary Teachers in England. Key Stages 1 and 2*. Norwich: HMSO.

Department of Education and Science/ The Welsh Office/Committee of Inquiry into the Teaching of Mathematics in Schools (1982) *Mathematics Counts: Report of the Committee of Inquiry into the Teaching of Mathematics in Schools under the Chairmanship of W.H. Cockcroft* (The Cockcroft Report). London: HMSO.

National Curriculum Council (1988) *Mathematics in the National Curriculum: A Report to the Secretary of State for Education and Science on the Statutory Consultation for Attainment Targets and Programmes of Study in Mathematics*. York: National Curriculum Council.

Singh, S. (1997) *Fermat's Last Theorem: The Story of a Riddle that Confounded the World's Greatest Minds for 358 Years*. London: Fourth Estate.

Upitis, R. *et al.* (1997) *Creative Mathematics*. London: Routledge.

Acknowledgements

I wish to thank Susan Davies, Jacqueline de Freitas and Emma Allanson for their help in writing this chapter.

CHAPTER 3

Science

Joyce Porter

GREENING THE RED PLANET: CAN PLANTS LIVE ON MARS?

I have been thinking hard about this, I have done some research and I think I have found an answer. I think plants can live on Mars. I don't mean that they are already living there; I mean that if you took a plant to Mars it could survive, with a little bit of help.

The air on Mars is full of carbon dioxide (95%) and it has a tiny amount of oxygen (0.2%) and a few other gases too. Plants use carbon dioxide to make food, and this makes oxygen. Plants also need sunlight, light and soil.

The sunlight is quite a bit less than on Earth, but in the summer the temperature can reach up to 17°C (63°F), but still the plant would need more sunlight, so that would have to be supplied.

The water is slightly less difficult but it still would be quite difficult. On Mars, there is actually water, but it is frozen. Some people say that in certain places, under the surface, is liquid water so you could get water on Mars.

I don't really know much about the soil on Mars but if it was impossible for a plant to live in the ground on Mars then soil from the Earth could be used.

It may seem that the plant wouldn't actually be able to live on Mars, because some things would be difficult to sort out, but I am saying that I think that, at a certain time of year, with some of the right technology, a plant may be able to live on Mars.

(Anna)

Anna, a ten-year-old, offered me this piece of writing spontaneously during a visit to her school. At the time I was working with her teacher to deliver some science lessons, which were unrelated to the topic of Earth in space. What does it tell us about the ability of science to inspire creative thinking?

Can we make links between Anna's work and the nature of scientific knowledge and scientific method? Monk and Dillon (2000) suggest that science can be perceived in a variety of ways: as a set of facts based on knowledge, which was established by eminent scientists in the past (in Anna's case a knowledge of how plants grow); it can also be seen as a set of logical and practical thought processes, which may result in research (research on the atmosphere of Mars) or skilled practical work, which can be defined by a set of instructions or be open-ended and investigative. Science may also involve the exploration of ideas which link to observation of a natural phenomenon or which arise from stimuli including investigative work, exploration that seeks to answer questions such as 'What is happening?'; 'Why does this occur?'; or 'How has this changed?' (Can plants live on Mars?). It is in this exploration of ideas that we see the main opportunity for stimulating creative thought. Anna demonstrated imaginative hypothesising and knowledge of how plants grow, supported by a process of research.

However, children's ability to think creatively and critically in science can only develop if it is nurtured in a classroom where they are cognitively and emotionally engaged (Matthews 2002). As Woolnough (1994: 9) states in his acknowledgement of exciting and stimulating science teaching,

> Doing science should be a holistic and not a reductionist activity. It should involve the affective as well as the cognitive aspects of a student's life. It is not only sufficient to be concerned with what students know and can do; one must also be concerned with whether they want to do it. It is of fundamental importance to develop students' emotional involvement with their work: to develop their motivation, their commitment, their enjoyment and creativity in science – for without these any knowledge and skills they acquire in the subject will be to no avail.

Without motivation, Anna would not have started to investigate her ideas about life on Mars.

Learning science is important for the future citizens of the world and so it forms a compulsory part of the curriculum at primary and secondary levels in many countries, but does the curriculum acknowledge the importance of stimulating creativity through science? The National Curriculum for England (2000) includes a reference to creativity:

> Science stimulates and excites pupils' curiosity about phenomena and events in the world around them. It also satisfies this curiosity with knowledge. Because science links direct practical experience with ideas, it can engage learners at many levels. Scientific Method is about developing and evaluating explanations through experimental evidence and modelling. **This is a spur to critical and creative thought**. Through science pupils understand how major scientific ideas contribute to technological change – impacting on industry, business and medicine, and improving quality of life. Pupils recognise the cultural significance of science and trace

its worldwide development. They learn to question and discuss science-based issues that may affect their own lives, the direction of society and the future of the world.

(Department for Education and Employment (DfEE) and the Qualifications and Curriculum Authority

(QCA 1999: 15)

That science and the scientific method are a creative endeavour is also emphasised in the science curriculum documents of many other countries.

Harlen (2000) argues that the teacher has a pivotal role in the success of any teaching and learning approach and this includes the promotion of creative and critical thinking in children. However, there are a number of reasons why some teachers do not allow creativity to flourish in their science lessons. The teacher's view of science teaching may be based on their experiences in school. This can result in them teaching science exclusively as a series of facts with an emphasis on basic principles:

> As a Year 6 teacher, my primary concern when teaching science was to ensure that the children had enough information, across a range of topics, to be able to tackle a variety of Key Stage 2 SATs questions. This was achieved simply by 'chalk and talk teaching', where I gave the children the information they required and they learnt it in rote fashion. The emphasis on practical science was minimal, as I believed it was a less successful method of imparting the large amount of information that the children required.

Such teachers may not have had the time to reflect on their own understanding of the nature of scientific activity and to review philosophies of science education. This is of crucial importance since the teacher's views of the nature of science and their understanding of how children learn science is likely to impact on the children in their classroom. Many teachers are faced with the daunting task of delivering all aspects of the science curriculum in an atmosphere dominated by the need for good Key Stage 1 and Key Stage 2 SATs results, and where the time to teach science has been reduced by the demands of the literacy and numeracy strategies. They may also lack confidence in their subject knowledge as many primary teachers have few qualifications in science above GCSE level (Ofsted 1999) and so feel less inclined to take risks.

Constructivism

Children arrive in the classroom with ideas and beliefs about how the world operates: ideas that have been formed from their own observations and experiences using their senses before their formal education begins. The importance of these 'alternative frameworks' or misconceptions in relation to teaching and learning has been recognised by many researchers (Driver *et al.* 1985; Driver *et al.* 1994). The constructivist view of learning is that the learner constructs his/her own knowledge. Their interpretations depend on prior ideas as well as the learning experiences provided.

The incorporation of science from 5–16 in the National Curriculum of 1988 acted as a stimulus for research activity in primary science. At primary level, the SPACE (Science Processes and Concept Exploration) project carried out at Liverpool University and King's College in the late 1980s and early 1990s was a major exploration of constructivist learning at primary level (Osborne *et al.* 1990; Russell and Watt 1990; Russell *et al.* 1991). Techniques involved: 1. understanding children's ideas; 2. helping children develop their ideas; and 3. moving the ideas forward to a more conventional scientific view. The research findings led to the development of the pupils' and teachers' materials of the Nuffield Primary Science Project (Wadsworth 1995).

If teachers can be encouraged to move from a transmission mode of teaching to an approach based on constructivism, then children will be encouraged to explore the world around them and to develop creative and critical thinking skills in a supportive environment. Research has shown this approach to be crucially important since many misconceptions can be retained into adulthood if left unchallenged (Carré 1993).

Establishing a non-threatening learning environment

If children are going to reveal their ideas confidently in front of their teacher and their peers, then the teacher has to set up a 'non-threatening' learning environment (Watts and Bentley 1987). This is an environment where learners, across the ability range, are willing to expose their ideas to others and have the confidence to suggest things, which are contrary to evidence, with the risk that their ideas may not work in practice. This takes time and is part of the relationship which exists between a teacher and the class and which extends across subjects. As Fisher (1990: 36) explains, 'The creative climate is maintained by communication, and communication is rarely neutral – either it helps to create an atmosphere where it is safe to share thinking and speculation or it damages that climate.'

A Year 6 teacher describes how she created such an atmosphere in her classroom:

> We established a climate where all were expected to contribute; it wasn't OK to sit back, and we employed strategies the children enjoyed. All contributions were welcomed – all contributions – and that was understood. It took time but that's the way of working, the ethos of the classroom anyway. And the questions I used, whilst being open, were also differentiated in terms of where people were. Ideas were never dismissed. In the beginning, when we looked at something new, we would write down every single idea

that people had, on the whiteboard, so everything was valued. To examine their ideas later, when we had looked at the evidence, we used pictures of light bulbs: if they agreed with the idea they held the light bulb up; if they did not agree, they did not hold it up.

In such an environment children freely express their views, as this discussion on condensation shows.

Sarah:	When the water vapour makes contact with a cold object, it condenses.
Teacher:	So, what do you think caused the change?
Sarah:	The water vapour's frozen.
Teacher:	Think about the words we used before – would any of those words help you to make your explanation clearer? Solid, liquid, gas . . . try to explain it again.
Sarah:	When the water vapour touches a cold solid, it turns back into a liquid.
Teacher:	And why does it?
Sarah:	It freezes and turns back into a liquid.
Teacher:	OK, so when this water evaporates from the beaker, it changes into water vapour, which is a gas, then Sarah says when it touches something cold like the window, Sarah says it condenses, it freezes – what would we see on the window if the water freezes?
Ben:	Ice.
Teacher:	Do we see ice on the inside of the window?
Children:	No.
Teacher:	What do we see?
Lee:	Like rain on the inside of the window.
Teacher:	And what do we call that – a solid, a liquid, or a gas?
Lee:	A liquid.
Teacher:	Yes, water is a liquid. So it doesn't freeze. Sarah, what would have to happen for the liquid to freeze?
Children:	It would have to be very cold.
Teacher:	So what is condensation?
Sarah:	Water vapour turns into a liquid.

The teacher involves several children in the discussion, exploring Sarah's understanding of the process of condensation and use of the correct scientific terminology. It is done with the empathy and support of the other members of the class. Building up a productive environment in the classroom in this way allows children to think positively about themselves, and encourages them to meet their creative potential.

Activities for exploration and involvement

The teacher needs to think creatively in choosing activities which are stimulating and will engage the children's interest. These activities can come from questions such as 'Why is the sky blue?' or 'What shape will hold the most marbles and still float?' The questions may arise from situations the children come across in real life, or they may be stimulated by posters, objects (such as a bicycle perhaps) and familiar stories: 'Was it sensible for Cinderella to be wearing glass slippers?' or 'Can you help Bob the Builder make strong foundations for his house?' There are also examples of scenarios which can be used to stimulate children's thinking, such as the four summarised below.

Scenario 1: predicting what will happen

The children observed shiny and dull materials and classified these. A significant number were unable to explain the connection between the shiny materials and reflection of light. The children were asked to predict what they would see if they were taken in small groups to examine three identical cardboard cats (one white, one black and one covered with aluminium foil) in a completely dark store cupboard.

Teacher: Will you be able to see the cats if we close the door and put the light out?
Jane: Yes, we will be able to see the shiny cat.
Teacher (to group): Do you agree?
Group: Yes, Miss.
Teacher: Why will you be able to see the shiny cat?
Tony: The light from our eyes will help us to see the shiny cat best.
Leanne: It is shiny.
Tom: It gives out light.
Teacher: Does that mean light comes from your eyes, then what?
Tony: It bounces off the shiny cat and comes back into our eyes.

Scenario 2: practical work involving observation

The children worked in groups; they were asked to consider what they would observe when ice pops are taken out of the freezer. (It was important that there was no frost on the outside of the ice pop wrapper initially, because this is one of the changes that happens, so they were wrapped in newspaper while in the freezer.) One child was asked to verify that there was no frost on the outside at the start. The children worked in groups to make observations over a period of time and write notes or single-word responses for anything they could sense, usually using sight and touch. Typically these were:

Joe: There is water on the outside.
Asif: It feels wet.
Emily: It feels like a liquid, water.
Sadika: It feels damp on the outside.
Asif: It's going frosty.
Emily: It's cold like ice.
Sadika: The frost's melting.

Richard:	It feels wet.
Asif:	It's gone softer.
Hannah:	It's gone.
Sam:	It's disappeared.

Scenario 3: use of concept cartoons

Concept cartoons (Naylor and Keogh 2000) are an excellent way of stimulating discussion about science concepts, particularly in situations where it is not possible to find evidence from carrying out investigative work in the classroom. Children work in groups to examine four ideas put forward in speech bubbles which provide them with uncertainty and cognitive conflict. They can discuss the ideas, find alternative explanations to the four offered and think of ways of finding the evidence to support their favoured idea. Children are again talking productively about science; they are clarifying their ideas and gaining a deeper understanding. The range of alternative ideas given on the concept cartoon reinforces science as a creative subject; there are different explanations for the same phenomena, there are new ideas to explore and consider and there may not be a single right answer.

Scenario 4: using a story

My name's Mrs Wobble – I am a cousin of Mr Bendy. I am all of a wobble because I've been given an important job of making jellies for the children's party at school. I don't know how I can do it because my eyes are too wobbly to read the instructions and my hand is too wobbly to hold a spoon – can you help me?

Reflecting on evidence

Language has a central role in developing a child's understanding, as thinking takes place in a social context, particularly through interactions between child and adult. Vygotsky (1978) argued that through the use of language children take control of their thinking and make meaning from the world. If peers, parents and teachers challenge a child's approach to a problem but then support the child by providing what Bruner called 'cognitive scaffolding' then the child's understanding can be extended. After children have experienced a practical situation – or perhaps discussed a concept cartoon as a group – and found some evidence for their ideas, it is important to create time to discuss their findings.

Scenario 1

The following reflections were offered after the children had been taken into the store cupboard (which was described above), initially with the light switched off, and then with a small amount of light entering the cupboard.

Teacher:	Could you see any cats when it was dark?
Group:	No, Miss.

Teacher:	Why?
Jo:	Because it was dark.
Billy:	There wasn't any light.
Teacher:	What happened when I let a small amount of light in the cupboard, could you see any cats then?
Group:	Yes, the shiny one.
Teacher:	Can you explain why you could see the shiny one?
Billy:	Because it's shiny.
Tony:	The light comes in from the door, reflects off the shiny cat into our eyes.
Teacher:	That's an interesting idea, do you agree with that? Jane . . .
Jane:	Yes, it comes in the door and bounces off the shiny cat into our eyes so we can see it.

Some children in the class worked out this explanation themselves, others were happy to accept their interpretation. After the activity, only one child in the class of 28 was not able to respond with the idea, 'light enters through the door, reflects best off the shiny cat and enters our eyes – that is why we can see the shiny cat'. The teacher encouraged the children to consider the new evidence from the activity, to listen to each other's thoughts, and hence extended their existing frameworks to develop their ideas towards a more conventional scientific view.

Scenario 2

Teacher:	Can you tell me where the frost, the ice on the outside, comes from?
Children:	There are tiny holes in the plastic that it gets through.
Teacher:	So you think the ice can get through the wrapper?
Children:	Yes.
Teacher:	So do you think that if we leave the ice pops overnight, all the liquid will have come out?

[Class put their hands up, half the class say yes, the other half say no. Those saying no have obviously thought carefully about eating ice pops and the fact that ice or melting ice does not usually leak out. In investigating the ice pops, inevitably one or two will start to leak, so the teacher makes use of this.]

Teacher:	Here is one that is leaking, what colour is the liquid that comes out?
Children:	Red [from a red ice pop].
Teacher:	What colour is the liquid when David wipes his finger on the one I have kept frozen?
Children:	Colourless.
Teacher:	So why is the liquid not red if it has come from the inside?
Matthew:	It has come from the air.
Teacher:	Why do you say that?
Chloe:	Water is in the air.
Teacher:	How do you know there is water in the air?

The teacher used practical evidence to extend the children's thinking. At this stage some children realised that the liquid on the outside of the ice pop was from the air. The dialogue continued with the teacher scaffolding the discussion further by encouraging some children to think about their previous experiences, such as observation of what happened when a kettle was boiled, or what happened when they breathed on a cold surface.

The examples show the essential role of language in science; the 'talk of science' (Leach and Scott 2000: 45) provides the conceptual tools for thinking about science. In listening to each other and to the teacher, each individual learner starts to relate the talk to their existing ideas, their previous experiences, and reflects on their thinking.

New ideas in new situations

If teachers encourage children to discuss and reflect on their experiences and evidence, then as they talk, they reveal ideas, which suddenly expose the extent of their understanding. Bruner (1964) developed the notion of creativity 'as an act of effective surprise'; when the new idea is stated, it seems so obvious and surprising in contrast to the ideas that were there before. Listening to children in classrooms reveals many effective surprises.

Scenario 5: children using a flexible strip of metal (1cm × 30cm) to explore the relationship between change in pitch and length

Raoul: When I vibrate the ruler very quickly, when it's short, I can feel the air particles above it vibrating too.

Henry: The air particles vibrate above the ruler, make more air particles vibrate; they reach my ear so I can hear the sound.

Scenario 6 (Year 6): children observing what happens when fizzy tablets (Alka-Seltzer) in water (in a closed bottle) are put on a balance

Yasmin: The bubbles could not come from inside the tablet because there were too many and they took up too much space and you cannot see them when you break the tablets open.

Scenario 7 (Year 2): children predicting what will happen when a toy car runs off a ramp

Sian: It will go further.

Abby: It will go faster.

Phillip: The higher the ramp, the faster the car will go.

Scenario 8 (Year 5): short circuit – wire from either end of battery to same connection on bulb

William: The bulb does not light but current still flows because it is connected to the battery via the bulb connector.

In her recent book, Harlen (2000: 13) has suggested that children's learning in science should 'start from the "small" ideas and build upwards so that at each point the ideas are understood in terms of real experience'. Primary science can then begin to enable children to make links between their experiences and build bigger ideas, as in the example below where Terry is reflecting after several lessons exploring the nature of dissolving, evaporation and condensation.

Teacher: Yes, Terry.

Terry: Miss, you know when the sea evaporates, Miss, the water vapour goes into the air, and the higher it gets the colder it gets – it forms clouds, and the salt, it can't evaporate so it stays down in the sea and when there is too much water vapour it'll turn back into water and form a cloud, so it rains.

Terry makes a leap of imagination in relating his practical investigations in class to the world of science outside the classroom, and also transfers knowledge from one scientific topic to another.

This application to a situation outside the classroom demonstrates a good understanding of the scientific constructs underpinning the topic under discussion. In discussing the water cycle, what happens to the salt in the sea is not normally considered, but Terry has inferred this from his investigation and has restructured his knowledge to contain a wider and more coherent set of ideas. The teacher then congratulates the pupil on making this link, and in doing so reinforces an important goal and sets a high expectation for all pupils in the class. Encouraging the children to question, debate and relate ideas is developing their thinking and conceptual understanding.

David George (1997) suggested the following are aids to creativity: listening to children, encouraging thinking skills, appreciating individuality and openness, encouraging open discussion, promoting active learning, accepting children's ideas and appreciating these ideas, allowing time to think and nurturing confidence. All of these facets are encouraged through a constructivist approach to science teaching.

Scientific enquiry

In the science enquiry attainment target of the National Curriculum, within the ideas and evidence strand, children learn to test ideas using observation and measurement. Within the investigative skills strand they plan, obtain, present and evaluate evidence. Both of these can be a powerful stimulus for creative thinking and independent learning. If the teacher allows an open-ended investigation to unfold, providing scaffolding at the appropriate moments, then children can develop their own investigations even at a very early age. An example is an activity which Year 3 children can carry out which explores different types of paper and their uses.

Groups of children are given samples of ten different types of paper: tissue paper, newspaper, card, transparent paper, kitchen roll, tracing paper, wrapping paper, etc., and they are asked to feel the textures of the different types of paper. The teacher then leads a discussion in which the children suggest what the different papers are used for and why. The teacher uses an example to stimulate thinking: 'I've bought my friend a brooch for her birthday; I wonder which paper will be best for wrapping it up. I want paper that does not crease. How do you think I can find out which paper creases the least?' The children answer her question and then suggest other properties they could investigate: strength, absorbency, transparency, flexibility, ease of tearing, so each group is planning their own investigation. The teacher facilitates the process by asking each group how they are going to carry out the task and by supporting their ideas.

The children carry out the practical investigations and, finally, each group produces a poster and explains their results to the rest of the class. Finally, they consider whether their investigation was successful, whether their predictions were correct and how they could improve what they had done.

Simple investigative activities such as this put science in a real context. To motivate children, 'the task must be meaningful in the sense that the child can conceive of a situation in which its performance would serve some real purpose, and, secondly, it must be challenging, not trivial, repetitive or wholly predictable' (Selley 2000: 30). Each group of children should be able to think of a situation where the findings of their investigation would be meaningful. They will know from their own experience that kitchen towels are good for mopping up water, but their investigation will demonstrate to them that newspaper could be used for this purpose in an emergency.

Investigative work can also stimulate imaginative cross–curricular activities. Primary teachers often use stories as an effective way to introduce investigations. In one investigation, which links with environmental concerns and citizenship, the teacher challenged the class to find a method to clean up part of the local beach where an old, rusty iron boat had been left. The children were asked to come up with ideas, and suggested filtering, using magnets and sieving. They discussed in groups which method would be best and decided to use magnets. After the children had successfully separated sand and iron filings using a magnet, the children then all wrote letters to the local council telling them how to clean up the beach. The science activity had stimulated literacy work, the results of which were made into an attractive display by the teacher. In another example, again as part of work on magnetism, the children made fridge magnets using small magnets embedded in plaster of paris poured into a mould such as a Christmas tree or Postman Pat van. The children then used their artistic skills to paint and varnish the magnets.

Extracurricular activities

Science clubs such as those run by teachers with the support of the British Association of Young Scientists (BAYS) clubs, are excellent examples of extra-curricular work in science and can be used to develop children's enthusiasm for science though problem-setting and problem-solving activities. As Bob Ponchaud (1998:18) says, 'there are strong indications that science thrives where extra-curricular activities are strong and varied'. Increasingly, these science clubs are being used creatively to deliver curriculum enhancement activities and have proven particularly motivating at primary level (Stanley 2002).

The BAYS bronze, silver and gold awards are designed as informal learning activies for young people under the age of 12 with the aim of helping young people to develop their curiosity towards an ability to investigate in a systematic way. The awards can motivate children of all ages and abilities and reward them for their efforts. As Chapman (2003) explains, 'the activities can light a spark in children precisely because they are not normal lessons'. The progression of a young investigator on the route from a bronze award to a gold award requires development of explicit investigative skills and is a very effective illustration of how these can be used to support the children's ability to explore their own creative ideas, to set themselves problems and investigate these in an increasingly more independent manner. As they progress and mature in age, teacher involvement to scaffold the building of skills, which are very similar to those in Scientific Enquiry, becomes less. At gold award level, the investigator sets his/her own problem and plans out the approach followed without any teacher involvement; it requires at least 30 hours' work.

In the first case study taken from examples provided by the BAYS, Alice and Lena's interest was stimulated by a local newspaper article about a child who had taken an overdose of iron tablets because he had mistaken them for sweets. Alice and Lena set up their investigation to find out:

(a) whether young children could differentiate between sweets and tablets which are commonly sold over the counter; and

(b) if all tablet containers are childproof.

They decided to carry out their project using children from primary school classes in Year 2, Year 4 and Year 6, so they had to ask permission from the parents for their children to take part and were required, then, to inform the children of the dangers of drugs.

The children were required to identify:

(a) which of the pairs of tablets and sweets on the board were drugs; and

(b) how difficult they found it to distinguish each pair.

Alice and Lena found that primary children, even those in Year 6, have problems identifying certain 'dangerous' drugs, which, if taken in excess, can kill. They also found that some of the pairs reported to be easy to differentiate were, in fact, done incorrectly. The participants were given three attempts to open each of five bottles; it was found that the paracetamol container was easy to open and that some tablets were not supplied in child-proof containers. Alice and Lena wrote a letter to sweet companies and drug companies outlining their results and putting forward recommendations on how to improve differentiation.

The children had worked creatively and collaboratively to identify a real-life problem to investigate. They designed their investigation systematically and worked in similar ways to real scientists. They were required to obtain parental permission (ethical approval) to carry out the research and they reported their results and made recommendations (published their work).

In the second case study Morgan was motivated by a series of advertisements seen on television and in magazines where different brands of toothpaste were claiming to have the best whitening properties. His aim was to test the truth of these claims. Morgan researched the structure of teeth and the common materials which stain teeth and then set up his experiment. His initial experiment used a set of teeth stained with tea with one half of each tooth covered in toothpaste and the other half left uncovered for several days. The results showed little difference between the various brands of toothpaste. So he designed a further experiment, which involved brushing the stained teeth using an electric toothbrush, but again there was no difference. So he carried out a third test in which the teeth were soaked in saliva before staining and brushing. At last, one brand of toothpaste appeared to be slightly better than the rest.

This case study shows Morgan used considerable ingenuity and persistence in devising a series of experiments which attempted to explore a real-life scenario. Again, there are parallels with the way real scientists work, as an enormous amount of thinking, experimentation and persistence is required to find the solution to problems.

Science across the curriculum

Combining science with other subjects such as poetry, art, drama, history and design & technology can help to simulate creativity. Science and technology can provide opportunities for solving real problems which involve thinking and doing. For instance, how can a large slab of rock be moved over several kilometres and then erected vertically in the ground as our ancestors did in the construction of monuments such as Stonehenge? (Geary 1987: 136).

In 2000, the Association of Science Education and Pfizer organised a very successful competition on science poetry writing. Over 13,000 entries were received. A selection of the best has been published in *Science Is Like a Tub of Ice Cream: Cool and Fun* (Feasey 2001). The following poem demonstrates divergent thinking about materials:

My Chocolate Teapot
Have you seen my chocolate teapot?
I left it on the jelly sofa
Maybe it's playing hide and seek with you and me
I lost it when I was washing the dishes with petrol
When I was standing next to the plastic window
Where was that strong smell coming from?
I was listening to the cotton wool radio
My dog was eating chunks of iron bars in his waxy candle bowl
Whilst lapping up caramel syrup
I was reading my glass cookery book
When my chocolate teapot disappeared.

(Shelley Joshi, Our Lady of Carmel Catholic Primary School, Doncaster)

Science is a creative subject, it provides many opportunities to stimulate children's creative and critical thinking. Children become more skilled in using their senses in exploring phenomena. Their motivation, problem-solving and feeling aspects of creativity prosper in a productive environment where they can put forward ideas and question the evidence. The challenge in teaching science is to provide children with experiences and the opportunity for dialogue in order to reflect and move their thinking from the intuitive to the scientific. A final thought from Rousseau (1762):

Teach your pupil to observe the phenomena of nature: you will soon rouse his curiosity, but if you would have it grow do not be in too great a hurry to satisfy this curiosity. Put the problems before him and let him solve them himself, let him not be taught science, let him discover it.

(*Emile*, bk 3)

Creative touches

- There are many ideas for creative activities on the Planet Science website (www.scienceyear.com). Explore all the sections including 'The Creative Classroom' – many of the resources can be downloaded. The site also links to a wide range of other useful science websites.

- Create a wild flower garden in the school grounds. Invite children to collect seeds or make suggestions about which plants should grow there. Children carry out research using observation of the local environment, books and the internet.

- Children observe the created habitat at different times of the year, collect and examine seeds, note the flowers produced and the insects and other animals which live in the garden.

- Design a flower for a specific purpose, e.g. to grow tall, to attract butterflies, to spread over an area.

- Model an animal which can survive in a particular habitat (Taylor and Jones 2001).

- Design an environment for the twenty-first century, e.g. what I need to live in space, underground, in the middle of the ocean, in a desert.

- Create a drama for a school assembly or presentation to parents, e.g. 'The Body Show' (Littledyke 2000).

- 'Pop rockets: How can I make my pop rocket go higher?' (Kibble 2001).

- Making a plaster of paris plaque. Ask the children to make a mould out of Plasticene 8–10 cm in diameter with a wall of 1–2 cm around it. Make a pattern in the Plasticene base by pressing the underside of a leaf or spaghetti shape into it.

- Catching the egg. Can your group make a structure out of ten pieces of A4 paper and 1 metre of masking tape that will catch an egg (raw) from 2 metres without it breaking? The winner is the team which uses least paper.

- Predict which fruit floats and which sinks. Test the fruits. Explain why.

- Create a mime based on pushes and pulls in various directions. Examine the forces involved: different ways of moving along the ground; tug of war. How can you make people speed up, slow down or change direction?

- How can you make a coloured shadow?

- Build the best kaleidoscope – use different numbers of mirrors; different end-pieces such as coloured marble or a rotating disc.

- Use a real-life graph to stimulate children's thinking about a science and society issue, e.g. the type of snacks eaten at break or the ways in which children travel to school compared with 1988 (Harwood and Porter 2002).

- Visit a science museum, or an industrial site. A list of science and discovery centres around the country is available from www.ecsite-uk.net.

- Invite a speaker in to talk about science.

- Organise a science week in the school with the children contributing ideas and setting up science displays and activities for other groups in the school, parents etc.

References

Bruner, J. (1964) *On Knowing: Essays for the Left Hand.* Cambridge, Mass.: Harvard University Press.

Carré, C. (1993) 'Performance in subject-matter knowledge in science', in N. Bennett and C. Carré (eds) *Learning to Teach.* London: Routledge.

Chapman, S. (2003) '21st century science clubs: enhancing the curriculum'. *Primary Science Review,* (submitted for publication).

Clark, B. (1988) *Growing Up Gifted.* Columbus, OH: Merrill.

Department for Education and Employment (DfEE) and the Qualifications and Curriculum Authority (QCA) (1999) *The National Curriculum: Handbook for Primary Teachers in England. Key Stages 1 and 2.* Norwich: HMSO.

Driver, R., Guesne, E. and Tiberghien, A. (eds) (1985) *Children's Ideas in Science.* Milton Keynes: Open University Press.

Driver, R., Squires, A., Rushworth, P. and Wood-Robinson, V. (1994) *Making Sense of Secondary Science: Research into Children's Ideas.* London: Routledge.

Duncan, S. and Bell, A. (eds) (2002) *The Little Book of Experiments.* London: Hodder and Stoughton.

Feasey, R. (ed.) (2001) *Science Is Like a Tub of Ice Cream: Cool and Fun.* Hatfield: ASE.

Fisher, R. (1990) *Teaching Children to Think.* Cheltenham: Stanley Thornes.

Geary, K. (1987) 'Science through technology', in R. Fisher (ed.) *Problem Solving in Primary Schools.* Oxford: Blackwell.

George, D. (1997) *The Challenge of the Able Child* (2nd edn). London: David Fulton.

Harlen, W. (2000) *The Teaching of Science in Primary Schools.* London: David Fulton.

Harwood , P. and Porter, J. (2002) *Handling Science Data Year 3, 4, 5 and 6.* Leamington Spa: Scholastic.

Kibble, R. (2001) 'Pop rockets: How can I make my pop rocket go higher?' *Primary Science Review,* 70: 11–12.

Klein, R. (1982) 'An inquiry into factors related to creativity'. *Elementary School* Journal, 82: 256–66.

Leach, J. and Scott, P. (2000) 'Children's thinking, learning, teaching and constructivism', in M. Monk and J. Osborne (eds) *Good Practice in Science Teaching: What Research Has to Say.* Buckingham: Open University Press.

Littledyke, M. (2000) 'Health and our bodies: using drama to enhance learning'. *Primary Science Review,* 65: 12–15.

Matthews, B. (2002) 'Why is emotional literacy important to science teachers?' *School Science Review,* 84: 97–104.

Monk, M. and Dillon, J. (2000) 'The nature of scientific knowledge', in M. Monk and J. Osborne (eds) *Good Practice in Science Teaching: What Research Has to Say.* Buckingham: Open University Press.

Naylor, S. and Keogh, B. (2000) *Concept Cartoons in Science Education.* Sandbach: Millgate House Publishers.

Ofsted (1999) *Primary Education: A Review of Primary Schools in England 1994–1998.* London: HMSO.

Osborne, J., Black, P., Smith, M. and Meadows, J. (1990) *Primary SPACE Report: Light.* Liverpool: Liverpool University Press.

Ponchaud, R. (1998) 'Quality in science education', in Sherrington, R. (ed.) *The ASE Guide to Primary Science Education.* Hatfield: ASE.

Revill, G. A. (2002) *Creative Science Activity Packs: Trees and Plants; Light, Dark and Colour; Minibeasts; Materials; Rocks; Predators.* London: David Fulton.

Russell, T., Longden, K. and McGuigan, L. (1991) *Primary SPACE Project Report: Materials.* Liverpool: Liverpool University Press.

Russell, T. and Watt, D. (1990) *Primary SPACE Project Report: Growth*. Liverpool: Liverpool University Press.

Selley, N. (1999) *The Art of Constructivist Teaching in the Primary School*. London: David Fulton.

Speedie, J. (2002) 'Using poems in primary science lessons'. *Primary Science Review*, 74: 19–20.

Stanley, E. (2002) 'Blades, bubbles and birds'. *Primary Science Review*, 71: 22–4.

Taylor, N. and Jones, P. (2001) 'Animal adaptation through modelling'. *Primary Science Review*, 66: 17–20.

Vygotsky, L.S. (1978) *Mind in Society: The Development of Higher Psychological Processes*. Cambridge, MA: Harvard University Press.

Wadsworth, P. (ed.)/Nuffield Primary Science (1995) *11 Teacher's Guides for KS1 and 11 Teacher's Guides for KS2*. London: Collins.

Watts, M. and Bentley, D. (1987) 'Constructivism in the classroom: enabling conceptual change by deeds and words'. *British Educational Research Journal*, 13 (2): 121–35.

Woolnough, B. E. (1994) *Effective Science Teaching*. Milton Keynes: Open University Press.

CHAPTER 4

D&T and ICT

David Spendlove and Matthew Hopper

Design and Technology (D&T) and Information Communication Technology (ICT, previously IT) evolved from one subject outlined in the first National Curriculum Order for Technology (Department of Education and Science and Welsh Office 1990). The main aim of both subjects is to prepare pupils for participation in a rapidly changing world using new technologies.

The creative aspects of D&T and ICT have been constrained by the increased emphasis on statutory assessment as part of the drive to raise standards in schools. Other recent national imperatives have also played a part in restricting the development of the D&T and ICT curricula as a consequence of the pedagogy which primary schools have been obliged to adopt. For example, the time taken for literacy and numeracy has reduced the time spent on D&T and ICT, subjects which benefit from sustained periods of work. However, since 1997 an increasingly vocal group of people has been drawing attention to the importance of providing opportunities for children to develop creative capability as part of their formal education.

> At a time when there is an emphasis on the basic skills of literacy and numeracy it is crucial to remind ourselves of the importance of creativity and imagination in their own right and in the contribution they make to other areas of learning.
>
> (Duffy 1998: 14)

Both D&T and ICT have evolved during a period of what has been unparalleled educational and technological change. As a consequence of the pace of this change the current form of these subjects has become confused and ill-defined, particularly when compared with other longer established foundation subjects such as history, geography, art & design, etc. There is also evidence to suggest that the focus of much of the work done in D&T and ICT has become increasingly 'outcome' rather than 'process' led, with insufficient focus upon the development of individual creative capability.

The subjects provide outstanding opportunities for 'high order engagement' as well as establishing an understanding of enterprise and industrial and commercial practice within a flexible and creative setting. They also provide opportunities for the application of knowledge gained from other subjects and a 'real world' context for subsequent learning. This chapter aims to consider where creativity exists within D&T and ICT and how teachers can capitalise upon best practice to provide meaningful learning experiences for pupils in both subjects.

Creativity in Design and Technology and ICT

Current thinking about D&T clearly shows the way that pupils' creativity should be centre-stage. Academic interest (Davies 1999; Kimbell 2002; Rutland 2002; Barlex 2003; Spendlove 2003) has chimed with an ongoing national debate about creativity in general, including the emerging theme of 'creativity in crisis' (Kimbell 2000a; Barlex 2003). In attempting to identify the unique educational components of Design and Technology, Harris and Watson (2003) draw attention to the academic and practical learning experiences that the subject has to offer and the interrelationship between conceptual (thinking) knowledge and procedural (doing) knowledge that underpins much of the work undertaken in schools. They describe Design and Technology as 'deliberately interdisciplinary' having its own 'distinctive non-verbal ways of thought' including the use of imagination and 'imaging'. We agree with Seltzer and Bentley (1999) that creativity is not an individual characteristic or an innate talent but is the application of knowledge and skills in new ways to achieve a valued goal, and as such, creativity is an ability that can be taught and nurtured.

A lack of emphasis upon the creative application of new technologies has been a problem for some ICT work. This has, in part, been due to an overemphasis on provision of digital resources at the expense of the rethinking of ICT capability and its potential application. The repercussions for this are that ICT is employed across many subjects, including D&T, but frequently its use lacks meaningful application of new technologies in creative ways, with the result that valuable opportunities to develop creative capability and to employ imaginative solutions to practical problems and challenges are frequently not exploited. ICT should be seen as a set of tools which can be adopted as and when appropriate to support and enhance creative processes. By providing new tools, media and learning environments, creative teachers can use ICT to support 'imaginative expression, autonomy, and collaboration, fashioning and making, pursuing purpose, being original and judging value' (Loveless 2002: 2).

The recent resurgence of interest in creativity in D&T and ICT and the considerable amount of research effort currently devoted to the field is as much a consequence of the demands of society (or more specifically commerce and industry) as it is a response to the stifling effects of the measuring and accountability culture that currently pervades education. Craft (2001: 1) has identified recent interest and research into creativity as going through clearly identifiable phases. In the 1980s and 1990s there was much academic interest in the identification and exemplification of a social-psychological framework, which was influenced by writers, including Gardner (1984), who focused predominantly upon the creative mind in terms of multiple intelligences (different ways in which learners might be considered 'smart'). Others, including Sternberg (1999), were driven by the needs of businesses and organisations who began to see the financial potential of creativity. More recently, accelerated learning approaches such as 'cognitive acceleration' and 'whole-brain' thinking strategies have become popular. Many such approaches have now been adopted nationally through initiatives such as the Key Stage 3 Strategy.

The extent to which the introduction of such approaches to teaching and learning has been of benefit in the drive to raise standards of learning achievement is unknown. However, the level of debate with regard to teaching methodologies, the different ways in which children learn and the place of creativity within formal learning is very welcome. This debate has also revealed that educators and policy-makers have widely varying views on the nature of creativity and the place it might occupy within formal education systems.

The links between creativity (and education in general for that matter) and increased economic performance remain unquestioned by politicians, as Tony Blair showed: 'Our aim must be to create a nation where the creative talents of all the people are used to build a true enterprise economy for the twenty-first century – where we compete on brains, not brawn' (National Advisory Committee on Creative and Cultural Education (NACCE) 1999: 6).

Both ICT and D&T have strong vocational links and play an important role in the shaping of future knowledge-based economies. D&T is very much orientated towards change in the made world which involves our clothes, food and infrastructure, while ICT is very much part of the 'invisible industries', shaping the rapidly developing 'e'-commerce sector of the economy. A common problem is the use of dated ideas about adoption of industrial practices within the classroom, which can constrain pupils' creativity in the subjects. Too often, existing industrial practice – rather than the future needs of industry – shapes the curriculum. Industrial constraints are ultimately a reality that can be experienced once students are working, but in school these should be minimised in order to nurture creative, forward-looking solutions to practical problems.

A further misconception is that primary practice should always mirror secondary practice. Kimbell *et al.* (1996) draw attention to the transition of pupils in D&T from the primary to the secondary curriculum and, in particular, pupils' progression (or regression) across the Key Stage 2/3 transition phase. Kimbell describes primary school experiences as typically empowered where the child has ownership of D&T activities and is enabled to make proposals and decisions within a supportive framework where the teacher acts as a consultant and a facilitator. This is contrasted with the same pupils' experiences within the first months of Year 7 (divided by only a six- week summer break) in the secondary school, where the experiences of the learner are characterised by the teacher acting as an instructor with the child being given limited ownership and little autonomy in the development of their work. In addition, unlike much good practice within the primary curriculum, the work often lacks context or coherence and does not build upon the valuable contributions which other subjects are able to make to the processes involved in designing and making. Such an approach loses sight of the essence of D&T and the rationale for its existence within the curriculum.

Opportunities for encouraging creativity in the classroom

The National Curriculum identifies some of the most important features of D&T in the 'statement of importance' (DfEE/QCA 1999:15) for the subject. Children will be prepared 'to participate in tomorrow's rapidly changing technologies' and 'learn to think and intervene creatively to improve quality of life'. The subject calls for pupils to become 'autonomous and creative problem-solvers, as individuals and as part of a team'. The statement concludes by saying that all pupils can become 'innovators'. This statement of importance represents a significant challenge for all teachers to nurture autonomy, creativity and problem-solving capability in the young learner. The ability to innovate requires pupils to develop their own range of skills, knowledge and personal qualities. Nevertheless, this challenge is entirely achievable if children are provided with an adequate and adaptable 'creative toolkit', which will enable them to aspire to this challenge.

It is important to explore first the context and conditions which will enable the challenge to be met. A critical factor for success is the need for teachers (either as individuals or as part of a team of professionals within a school) to establish a clearly defined, theoretically rigorous framework within which children might be encouraged to work towards the development of creative capability. Our own experience has shown that where there is a shared vision and philosophy for the teaching of D&T and ICT within a school, children are able to flourish and to frequently exceed the initial expectations of their teachers.

In order for creativity to be achieved there needs to be a measure of uncertainty and a level of risk-taking. Indeed, without uncertainty there can be no creativity and without risk-taking there can be no innovation. Schools and teachers need the security and 'licence' that are provided by a carefully considered whole-school approach to the teaching of creative capability where uncertainty and risk-taking are accepted components of creative work. However, without adequate theoretical underpinning including the establishment of a carefully considered and effective philosophy within which creativity can flourish, the strategies offered later in this chapter merely become a 'quick fix' or 'tips for teachers', an approach which has previously prevented rather than enabled teachers to effectively respond to the challenge we described above.

Creative processes: the quest for an effective model

Engineers, educationalists and others frequently refer to the 'design process' or 'creative process' as if it were a universally accepted model for the resolution of design problems and/or the creation of artefacts, systems, products and environments – it is not. 'Pupils are too frequently forced to design to a formula called "The Design Process". This redundant model is still seen by many as the only legitimate design tool' (Downie *et al.* 1997: 254). Such models are characterised by a rigidly linear approach and tend to begin with the identification of a need or want, and systematically (and some would say mechanistically) progress through a series of stages called, typically, 'ideas generation', 'design development', 'specification', 'realisation' and (curiously, since it implies this is a discrete activity to be carried out at the completion of a design activity) 'evaluation'. This does not adequately describe the complex intellectual and practical human activity which we call 'design'. Such human activity requires the sophisticated application of skills, knowledge and value judgements to be made at each stage of a complex process. This is as true of the child designing a spreadsheet as it is of the architect involved in the design of an international airport.

Contrast such an approach with that advocated by Richard Kimbell: 'Designerly thinking is both creative and evaluative and from the very moment that we start to tackle a task the iterative process of action and reflection – thought in action – is the fundamental modus operandi' (Kimbell 2000b: 3). Kimbell's ability to succinctly describe process within the subject field of Design and Technology is impressive as it encapsulates the relationship between thinking and doing and clearly implies a sequence of activities that are fluid, speculative and which are likely to result in a range of possible outcomes rather than only a predetermined 'product'.

There have been many attempts to graphically represent the processes involved in creative decision-making and design. However, the model illustrated as Figure 4.1 is particularly successful as it acknowledges that the brain is at work and implies the need for uncertainty, reflection and the employment of creative intuition in the resolution of a design challenge. This model also implies a high level of engagement on the part of the learner and an expectation

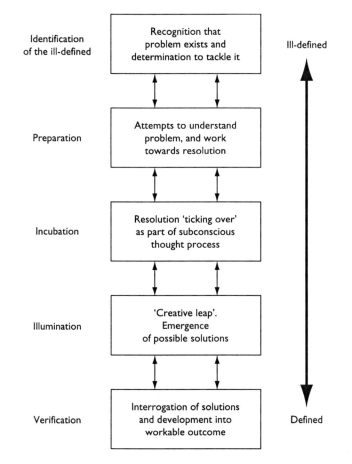

Figure 4.1 Creative design process model

that the thinking involved transcends both the orthodox and the confines of the school day. It is our own experience that where there is purposeful engagement and genuine challenge, then the learner will continue to propose solutions and to ask 'What if' beyond the time designated for such activities in school.

In Figure 4.1 the different stages are visited and revisited as ideas are formed, developed and refined. The model also implies that there is no expectation at the outset that there will be a fully defined outcome in the form of a 'product'. Instead, the expectation on the part of both teacher and learner is that the outcome is the growth in capability which has resulted from an involvement in a creative challenge.

Factors influencing creativity in the classroom

We now identify some other key factors that need to be considered when planning experiences which aim to develop children's creative abilities. However, no checklist, model or package can create the truly creative experience. This requires the discernment, reflection and insight of 'reflective practitioners', which are features of a good match between pupil needs and teacher practice. As Marks-Tarlow (1996: 10) points out, 'creativity is a maturational process' which unfolds through the inborn ability and (crucially in our view) 'exposure to encouragement, opportunities and respected role models'.

Recognising creative children

Children who bring a high level of creative capability to a task do not always realise that they have particular ability. Highly creative children can often seem awkward or difficult as they may appear to be challenging the norm of the classroom. It also has to be recognised that all children are creative in some way and that it may not be just those children who have common creative traits or who are good at the conventionally creative subjects.

Generally, creative children may have a sense of curiosity and wonder, are inventive (even with excuses!), flexible, imaginative and original. Creative children are also often willing to take risks, can tolerate ambiguity and may occasionally break boundaries. Occasionally, creative children may be considered difficult because they can be independent and nonconformist, are knowledgeable of social rules and can operate close to the edge. This should be considered as a strength rather than as a weakness.

When judging creative capability the teacher needs to consider both the individual and the environment in which the individual is working. A child may come up with ideas that are unique to them, for which they should be praised, but are well-known to others, which may detract from the novelty of the ideas. Prior learning and environment always have to be considered when recognising and rewarding the creative individual. Above all, it is important to keep in mind that 'All children are born with creative ability but it is up to us to provide a climate to support the child's creative efforts' (Fisher 1990: 34).

Creative children may not always be high achievers in terms of statutory tests as they may be easily distracted or bored. There is some evidence that it may even be a disadvantage to be creative in secondary schooling as creativity is not assessed by examination boards, and therefore children can become frustrated by their lack of success when they feel they should be achieving much more.

Risk-taking

Pupils must be able to manage risks and to learn from mistakes. Opportunities for exploration and play without fear of making mistakes within a non-threatening environment provide the optimum creative learning experience. This approach does not promote recklessness but recognises that highly constrained, predetermined activities with little opportunity for pupil 'owner-ship' are unlikely to foster creative capability. Too often the attempt to produce 'quality products' is at the expense of quality thinking, uncertainty and risk:

> The central feature of designers' thinking is the recursive relationship between projective thinking (into the future) with reflective thinking (on the impact of the projection). Designing involves creative exploration of the new and unknown and (at the same time) reflection on this new state, in terms of how we got there, why we got there, whether or not we have been successful.
>
> (Kimbell 2000b: 3)

By purely focusing upon outcomes (quality products), the value of exploring, designing, innovating, communicating and taking risks can be lost. It has to be remembered that there is real validity in not finishing a project. How else do children learn about time-management skills or the consequences of over-ambition? There is also genuine value in not being sure if something is going to work and whether an idea is possible (even though this may be uncomfortable for the teacher and the pupil). Experimenting and notional 'failure' are essential features of a positive creative experience.

Persistence and determination to find new ideas

A willingness to take on what appear to be difficult tasks characterises creative learning. Smith (2001) identifies how the brain responds best to conditions of high challenge together with low stress where there is learner choice and regular feedback. In order for children to develop the ability to explore new ideas and to constantly ask themselves the question 'what if?' they must be allowed the time for reflection and the space to explore new ideas, to add value to their thinking and to work this through into tangible outcomes that might be further evalu-ated. Predetermined outcomes merely deny opportunities for the child to develop their creative capability.

> The mark of the critical thinker is the readiness to challenge the ideas of others. This means that if we wish our children to be critical thinkers then we should try to encourage their challenges to our ideas and ways of thinking.
>
> (Fisher 1990: 67)

There are many ways in which children can be encouraged to re-work their ideas and visualise solutions to design problems in different ways. Edward de Bono employs a technique which he calls PMI (plus, minus and interesting), which when used with children encourages them to push back the boundaries of their thinking and to add value to their ideas.

Approaches like this facilitate an 'internalised dialogue' or what we frequently describe to our own students as a 'dialogue with oneself' which can also be

Put the idea or object here	Write positve comments about the idea or object (the pluses here)
Write all the interesting things here	Write the negative (the minuses) here

Figure 4.2 Edward de Bono's Plus, Minus, Interesting (PMI) technique

Figure 4.3 Worked example of PMI

replicated as a dialogue between learners and their teacher and/or peers. This opportunity to talk (internally or externally) and to explore ideas is an essential prerequisite to the development of new and novel solutions to problems. Talking – especially the type which helps young people to handle new ideas, deal with uncertainty, develop reasoned arguments and internalise experiences in order to find personal expression for them – is a critical and often undervalued activity in the D&T and ICT environment. Such talk facilitates problem-solving and enables children to explore cause and effect and to evaluate their options.

Playfulness

A key condition of creativity is the opportunity for the incubation of new and novel ideas. This implies recognising play or playfulness as integral to developing new ideas and is consistent with the promotion of risk-taking. If we recognise that failure is part of the process then it must be accepted that time has to be allocated to playing with ideas in order to reject some and develop others. The notion of play need not be completely unstructured as there are a range of methods which can be employed to structure play, such as the example of 'walking on the wild side' (see Figure 4.4).

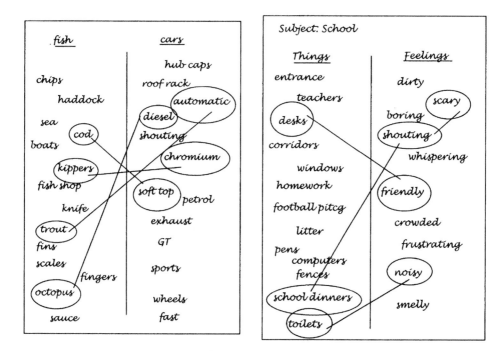

Figure 4.4 Edward de Bono's 'Walking on the Wild Side'

'Walking on the Wild Side' makes sense out of random associations and is a way of deconstructing conventional thinking while facilitating idea generation. Themes, which may be chosen by the teacher or the learner, have words randomly associated to them and then links are made between the two discrete themes to come up with unusual associations which form the basis of the next design iteration. Many of these methods exist (including SCAMPER, Six Hats, 50 circles, etc.) which can be used to free up thinking while providing structured playfulness. The adoption of these methodologies is ideally suited to the respective D&T and ICT strands of 'Designing' and 'Developing ideas and making things happen'.

Recent software developments in ICT and D&T also provide real opportunities for playfulness through modelling, simulating, exploring and monitoring ideas which previously were often inaccessible to children due to cost and technical requirements. Primary school children can now speculate and take risks with computer-aided design (CAD) or modelling software without fear of damage or without fear of constraint by limiting factors such as size, cost or space.

Case study

A PGCE student asked a Year 6 class to design a digital camera for use by young children. The student had a background in product design and came to the task with no preconceptions or particular expectations with regard to outcomes. It was her first experience of working with children at Key Stage 2 and the only advice we offered was that she should approach the work from the perspective of a product designer working with novice designers rather than as a teacher working with a group of pupils. She was further encouraged to introduce the design methodologies she had employed in her professional work to children and to share exemplary design work with them. The result was a range of individual design proposals, which challenged the current orthodoxy in camera design.

The children were given opportunities to use digital cameras and to reflect upon the various features they offered and to prepare a critique in terms of their suitability for use by younger children. The children then experimented with function and form employing CAD software (Techsoft 2D) and went on to create sketch-models from foam, card and other materials which they subsequently photographed and further modified using image manipulation software. This enabled the children to quickly make changes to their proposals and to make judgements about the size, proportions and colour of their design proposal and/or to focus upon one aspect of the design such as the controls or a novel feature.

The strength of the approach lies in the pace at which ideas can be processed. Ideas can also be communicated quickly to others for group discussion, comment and feedback and, as they were in this example, tried out with the potential end-users who provided invaluable insights for subsequent design development. Such insights included the importance of colour – pastel shades were thought by six-year-old children to be 'babyish'. The young 'consumers' also had clear ideas of what they expected from a camera and made it clear that they required high levels of sophistication in terms of the features offered.

The outcomes of the activity were original and innovative and included the suggestion of printing out images directly from the camera. This in turn resulted in a debate about the form of the camera and the need to include some of the characteristics of a printer in terms of stability, paper storage, etc. Other innovations included the ability to directly manipulate images before printing, enabling the user to put their teacher or their dad behind bars or make their cat purple! One design proposal was for a robust, lightweight camera that could be thrown in the air to enable the user to take aerial photographs. The presentation sheet (Figure 4.5) shows some of this thinking.

The children were fully engaged in the design activity in a way that reflected modern professional design processes. They were also not restricted by a requirement to complete a fully functioning manufactured 'product'.

Nevertheless, the children were provided with opportunities to employ a broad range of tools (including ICT tools), materials, media and technologies to formulate, modify, model and present their ideas.

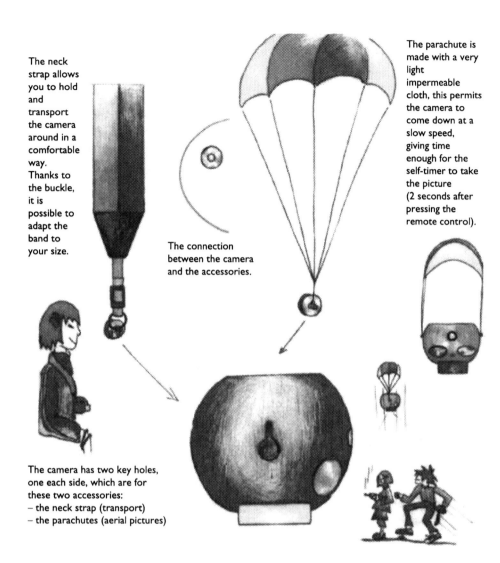

The neck strap allows you to hold and transport the camera around in a comfortable way. Thanks to the buckle, it is possible to adapt the band to your size.

The parachute is made with a very light impermeable cloth, this permits the camera to come down at a slow speed, giving time enough for the self-timer to take the picture (2 seconds after pressing the remote control).

The connection between the camera and the accessories.

The camera has two key holes, one each side, which are for these two accessories:
– the neck strap (transport)
– the parachutes (aerial pictures)

Figure 4.5 Child's design for a lightweight camera

Appropriate learning environments

D&T and ICT often require specific learning environments that can be used flexibly at different stages of the creative process to make the most of learning opportunities. Often the preoccupation with having the latest technology, such as the latest white (elephant?) board, can become a distraction from the learning that may or may not take place. Nevertheless, traditional settings for both subjects are continually challenged as new technologies impact upon what and how we teach. The introduction of CAD and computer-aided manufacture (CAM) and the introduction of more sophisticated software (e.g. computer-aided learning (CAL)) and wireless networks can create new opportunities and environments for delivering the subjects creatively. It must be stressed, however, that the most important resource is a capable and reflective teacher.

The time for introduction of new technologies and hence the time for embedding them meaningfully in the curriculum is, increasingly, being shortened. Opportunities for reflection prior to the introduction of these technologies are also decreasing. Both subjects have suffered from innovation 'on the go' and will increasingly continue to do so as new technologies find their way onto the curricula. Productive environments which promote creativity tie in all the essential elements discussed within this chapter including opportunities for risk-taking, exploration, play, flexibility, reflection, as well as providing appropriate stimulus, access and space.

How do we know if such productive environments have helped learning? It is easier to assess pupils' application of skills and techniques in D&T and ICT than it is to assess creative interpretation or application. Often the inherent creative opportunities of the subjects are restricted by externally imposed assessment procedures which fail to adequately recognise creativity. The primary National Curriculum programmes of study for D&T and ICT are meant to encourage creativity yet the levels of attainment fail to acknowledge creativity in any way. Teachers must therefore be reflective in making their own judgements; to fail to encourage, recognise, and promote creativity simply because of the inadequacies of statutory testing would be damaging.

The current resurgence of interest in creativity is, hopefully, not just a 'fad'. Creativity is central to the cultural life of all societies and, as such, we need to nurture, promote and understand it. The effective teacher of D&T and ICT is an explorer, a thinker, an information manager, a collaborator, a facilitator and a partner in providing a rich learning experience for children. When this is the case, then the learner is also encouraged to take on these roles. The heart of this learning is the opportunity for learners to interrogate their surroundings intelligently and to imagine alternatives to the existing 'made' environment. Ultimately, we must recognise that children have the capability to be creative and to challenge the orthodox, including our own ideas:

> One of the challenges of teaching children to think is to help them to discover that the process of evaluating, approving and disapproving of one's ideas is natural and healthy; the confidence to be self-critical can strengthen the sense of self.
>
> (Fisher 1990: 67)

Creative touches

- Foster curiosity. Seek to foster curiosity by collecting and displaying unusual products. A good lesson starter is asking children to speculate on what an object might be used for. Encourage wild ideas.

- Challenge those children who want to stifle creativity particularly when doing group work (see de Bono's six hats). When they say an idea is 'silly', challenge them about their thinking (the BBC has recently introduced a yellow card which can be waved at staff who are blocking creative ideas).

- Encourage pupils to take risks, manage risks and learn from their mistakes. This includes encouraging pupils to have a willingness to try difficult tasks as well as supporting pupil persistence and determination to find new ideas.

- Display the characteristics you wish your pupils to develop. Merely hoping your children will become creative is insufficient. You have to have confidence in your own abilities and adopt the same creative characteristics that you promote.

- Encourage children to make links across their different learning contexts. Design and Technology and ICT are subjects that are highly dependent upon using information from other subjects. Therefore children must not create barriers which prevent them from applying information naturally.

- Encourage a desire for novelty. Encourage children to search for novel ideas in magazines and on websites. Compile scrapbooks of novel ideas that can be used to inspire. Collections of novel products on display also promote speculation from children as well as providing stimulus when creating.

- Encourage an atmosphere in the classroom that is free from domination by external rewards. Although we exist in an 'assessment culture' not everything has to be assessed all of the time. Certain aspects of creativity are very difficult to assess in summative ways; therefore consider recognising achievement through celebrations and displays.

- Encourage playfulness. Playing with ideas is an important feature of being creative. It has to be appreciated that not all ideas will come to fruition but the process of playful speculation is an important one.

- Encourage children to use both sides of their brain, e.g. the verbal and the non-verbal, the rational and non-rational. It is important that when children are designing language is involved. Getting children to 'talk through' how their ideas have developed makes links within the brain.

- Challenge every assumption – try to dismantle children's ill-informed assumptions about designing products, e.g. that new products are always better, that buildings shouldn't move and that using computers is always better.

- Try the following websites:
  Tracey Beaker http://www.bbc.co.uk/cbbc/tracybeaker/
  Sodaplay http://wwwsodaplay.com
  Design and Technology Association http://www.DATA.org.uk

Design Council www.designcouncil.org.uk

West Point bridge builder software http://bridgecontest.usma.edu/download.htm

Creative toys www.toysymphony.net

Using Macromedia™ with primary school pupils www.tygh.co.uk/creativity_in_ICT.html

www.naction.org.uk/creativity/index.htm

References

Barlex, D. (2003) 'Creativity in crisis: design and technology at KS3 and KS4'. DATA Research Paper 18. Wellesbourne: Design and Technology Association.

Craft, A., Jeffrey, B. and Leibling, M. (2001) *Creativity in Education*. London: Continuum.

Davies, T. (1999) 'Taking risks as a feature of creativity in the teaching and learning of design and technology'. *Journal of Design and Technology Education*, 4(2): 101–8.

Department for Education and Employment (DfEE) and the Qualifications and Curriculum Authority (QCA) (1999) *The National Curriculum: Handbook for Primary Teachers in England. Key Stages 1 and 2.* Norwich: HMSO.

Department of Education and Science and the Welsh Office (DES/WO) (1990) *Technology in the National Curriculum.* London: HMSO.

Downie, M., Hopper, M. G., Fowler, A. and Thistlewood, D. (1997) 'Innovation in schools', in J. S. Smith (ed.) *International Conference on Design and Technology Education Research and Curriculum Development.* Loughborough: Loughborough University.

Duffy, B. (1998) *Supporting Creativity and Imagination in the Early Years.* Buckingham: Open University Press.

Fisher, R. (1990) *Teaching Children to Think.* Cheltenham: Stanley Thornes.

Gardner, H. (1984) *Frames of Mind: The Theory of Multiple Intelligences.* New York: Basic.

Harris, M. and Watson, V. (2003) *Designs on the Curriculum? A Review of the Literature on the Impact of Design and Technology in Schools in England.* Brief No. 41. London: DfES.

Kimbell, R. (2000a) 'Creativity in crisis'. *Journal of Design and Technology Education*, 5(3): 206–11.

Kimbell, R. (2000b) *Critical Concepts Underpinning the Design & Technology Curriculum in England.* Keynote address, International Technology Education Conference, Germany. University of Brunswick.

Kimbell, R. (2002) 'Assessing design innovation: the famous five and the terrible two', DATA International Research Conference 2002. Wellesbourne: Design and Technology Association.

Kimbell, R., Stable, K. and Green, R. (1996) *Understanding Practice in Design and Technology.* Buckingham: Open University Press.

Loveless, A. (2002) *Literature Review in Creativity, New Technologies and Learning.* NESTA Futurelab.

Marks-Tarlow, T. (1996) *Creativity Inside Out: Learning through Multiple Intelligences.* Menlo Park, CA: Addison Wesley Publishing.

National Advisory Committee on Creative and Cultural Education (NACCCE) (1999) *All Our Futures: Creativity, Culture and Education.* Suffolk: DfEE.

Rutland, M. (2002) 'What can we learn about creativity from professional designers to inform design and technology classroom practice?' DATA International Research Conference 2002. Wellesbourne: Design and Technology Association.

Seltzer, K. and Bentley, T. (1999) *The Creative Age: Knowledge and Skills for the New Economy.* London: Demos.

Smith, A. (2001) 'What the most recent research tells us about learning', in F. Banks and A. Shelton-Mayes (eds) *Early Professional Development for Teachers*. London: David Fulton Publishers.

Spendlove, D. (2003) 'Gendered perceptions of creativity and design and technology', in E. Norman and D. Spendlove (eds) DATA International Research Conference 2003: Wellesbourne: DATA.

Sternberg, R. J. (1999) *Handbook of Creativity*. Cambridge: Cambridge University Press.

CHAPTER 5

Humanities

Russell Jones and Jo Dennis

For the purposes of this chapter, the humanities are largely represented by the subjects history and geography. There is, of course, a much better definition of this curriculum area (English is covered separately in another chapter), but the intention of the authors is that the points made here apply broadly across the whole range of the humanities subjects. Like other primary subjects, the humanities benefit from opportunities to encourage children to become active and productive in their own progression. A recent project found that: 'Young peoples' creativity seems to flourish when their learning environment values diversity, encourages them to experiment and take risks, and offers trusted guidance, respect and support' (Rawling and Westaway 2003: 9). This is not, however, to suggest that pupils are merely sent away to 'teach themselves', or that the processes involved in the business of creative teaching and learning are not rigorous and focused. The same piece of research concluded that: 'young people are most creative when constraints are given – a time limit, a word limit, a limit on resources – than when an activity is completely open ended' (*ibid.*: 9).

The good teacher of humanities in the primary school understands that creativity needs to be part of the teaching and learning environment, but that this does not happen by chance and it is unlikely to happen when there is over-prescription. There is a careful balance to be struck where pupils can be encouraged to take risks and to explore personal avenues of interests, but where the teacher can maintain an overview of progression and development.

Geography and history are particularly interesting starting points for creative teaching and learning because the teacher has clear and immediate openings through which the child can be engaged. Once recognised, there is a joy to this process that other subjects on the primary curriculum struggle to match. The first opening is to bring every child into the selected area of study by looking at similarity and difference. It does not particularly matter what area of study is selected. The pupil instantly has the opportunity to begin an exploration along the lines of:

- How is this different to *my* life *now*?
- Are there any similarities between the ways the Victorians (for example) organised their school days and the way *my* school day is organised *now*?
- How is this climate different to the climate at home?
- Why were the clouds on my holiday different to the clouds I usually see at home?

It was acknowledged a century ago that the child needs to be engaged if deep, meaningful learning is to be achieved, and we would argue that this is still central to the creative processes necessary for the modern primary child:

> The child's interest must be won [by] an incident and event that arouses him [sic], as we can see quite clearly in his games, where he loves to be acting ... however the ultimate aim need not be forgotten. We can teach a child to reason, even when we are telling him a story.
>
> (Neild 1907: 290–1, cited in Bage 2000: 11)

It may sound simplistic but by bringing in these kinds of questions at an early stage of a geography or history study, the teacher immediately offers the child an engagement point; instead of the subject being distant in location and/or time, pupils are invited to look for links specific to their own life experiences.

Geography

Children are naturally interested in themselves and the world around them. These two interests come together within geography, a subject that naturally bridges both the arts and sciences. Geography invites a variety of rich starting points through questions children can raise themselves:

- Where do people live?
- How do people live their lives?
- What do they do?
- Why do they do it that way?
- What is their environment like?
- Has it been modified by man?

To harness and excite children's interest invites a creative form of teaching that engages their senses in different ways to give depth of understanding within investigation and learning.

Geography is a wonderful cross-curricular vehicle for giving children an integrated view of their world. It can be great fun and can involve children in a highly interactive way in which they can partly guide the content of their work – giving them commitment to and ownership of their geography projects. A cross-curricular approach to geography does not need to ignore the National Curriculum programme of study. It should not be seen as a constraint but as an opportunity to focus closely on issues and ideas that are specific to the subject of geography while ensuring effective progression through the syllabus.

For example, a clear cross-curricular opportunity in this context is the potential offered by ICT to the study of geography. Recent developments in ICT have given teachers and children the power to access a huge field of electronic information from their classrooms. Once located, there is enormous creative potential for teachers to work alongside children in deciding how this information is used, what other questions have been raised (and how they might now be answered) and what form of study will develop out of these findings.

The QCA Creativity Project (Qualifications and Curriculum Authority 2003) found that the two key emphases which geographical work brings to creativity are:

● the focus on interpreting and understanding place and environment; and

● the use of maps, graphical representations and visual images, often alongside text.

Case study

A Year 4 class began to study 'Villages'. The school is located in a suburban council estate on the outskirts of an industrial town. Many of the children had little personal experience of village life but were interested to learn about this. The school is fortunate in having a new building, opened in 2001, and excellent ICT facilities. The classroom has an interactive whiteboard which is connected to the internet. There is a computer suite with 17 networked computers allowing the children to sit two to a computer. The starting point was to examine what their town had to offer – its facilities, services and general appearance. In a question-and-answer session, lists of features in the town were compiled.

Using the interactive whiteboard the children looked at a map of the local area on www.multimap.com. They noticed the density of the roads and buildings. They were fascinated by the aerial photographs which showed their homes and streets. They were able to access historical maps and photographs showing the development of the town. When they visited the computer suite they were able to enter their own postcodes and see detailed maps of their own group of streets. The facility to enter different scales to view maps gives immediacy to the understanding of mapping scales. The ability to navigate through the main points of the compass supports learning about direction. This process embedded the children's thoughts about towns so that they could better understand the contrast with the villages to be found in the countryside.

The next visit to the internet site was to look for comparative information on villages. As the teacher lives in a Welsh village the children were encouraged to enter her postcode and look at her village. The children were asked what they thought they might find there. From their previous knowledge of towns lots of ideas were contributed and they were surprised to find that there was only a primary school, one shop, a post office, a church, a village hall, a scout hut and two pubs. They noticed from the aerial photograph that green fields came almost to the heart of the village and that there were very few roads with houses.

The children then interviewed the teacher about life in her village. As it is within striking distance of towns with good facilities, they learnt that just as they would travel to a town centre to access large shops, cinemas, libraries and hospitals, the teacher would drive to the town to do the same thing. It was explained that some villages were much more remote and so the decision was made to try to find some of these.

The children looked at atlases and maps of Great Britain, searching for the names of places that might be villages. They considered features such as the lack of major roads, the absence of large towns, the smallness of the location mark and of the print. On multimap.com and also streetmap.com you are able to find maps by entering a place name instead of a postcode. In the computer suite they entered the names of places they had found. There was delight when they found tiny villages in different parts of the country.

Once back in the classroom again, plans were made to make a model village. Each child was given a small piece of paper – about 10 × 15 cm – and asked to draw a building for the village. Textbooks and pictures about buildings and the countryside were on hand to provide inspiration. Help with ideas was given freely so that everyone became proud of their house. Several children offered to draw other village buildings – the church, the village hall and rather a lot of pubs! The class discussed whether we had enough public buildings and spaces. Would there be a playground or a village pond? Was there a village green where you could play games? How about a wood – there is a wood on the school field that the children planted a few years ago? We discussed the needs of the people living in the village. Who would there be? Most places have children, but would there be enough to justify a school? Where would the old people live when they couldn't manage on their own in a big house? Perhaps there would be old people's bungalows. The children were also given large sheets of white paper and, in groups of three or four, asked to plan a village. There was good discussion between the children about where everything should go and who lived where.

A display board at the front of the classroom was covered. The teaching assistant glued cut-outs of roads onto the 'map' as the children made suggestions to her. A simple network emerged. Children were then asked to choose a location for their buildings. Some debate arose about how many pubs could go in and what to do with two churches. A brief discussion about planning regulations followed. The children were told that, unlike in the past, it was no longer possible to just build a house – you had to have planning permission from the local authority and build according to certain standards. A very successful drama activity can be to ask the children to act as a local council and debate whether to allow a new development or refuse it – perhaps a mobile phone relay station, a car park, a caravan site or a tip for the rubbish from the nearby town.

To develop the village layout every child drew a tree and painted it. The trees were added to form woodland at the edge of the village. Two ponds were painted with a swan or two. There was also a football pitch, as life could not be contemplated without one! A suggestion list was used to name the roads and the children voted for the favourites – they had discovered that 'Lane' was often used to name small country roads. There would be the chance to investigate the origin of street names with older children.

However remote the village, it had to have road signs, and in the next art lesson the children designed signs to go all over the village. Many were decorated with designs suggesting the natural world. The children discussed whether the use of transport would be the same as in a town. What sort of vehicles would be used? How often would buses run? This could lead to a study of timetables, comparing a rural service with an urban one. The children could decide which residents owned different vehicles and create a graph or a database to record the information for analysis.

Many children chose to draw and colour their own maps for fun, creating new village layouts. Some tried using graphical drawing tools and stamps on programs such as *Colour Magic* and *My World 3*. They were encouraged to add a key, a compass rose and a scale bar. Several children started to design new buildings as homes or village amenities.

The geography work overflowed into the Literacy Hour. A simple questionnaire was designed for the children that they each filled in. It asked them about the people who lived in the house they had drawn to encourage them to think about personalities and other people's lives. With their notes in front of them they surveyed the map of Brookside village (named after the school and not the TV programme). The class began to describe the inhabitants of the village. Slowly, children began to interact, suggesting that someone in their house was friendly with a neighbour. We learnt that one person had to travel a long way to work and wasn't home very much except at weekends. Quite a group met at the football field and later went to The Bull to chat. The younger children could go to school in the village but the older ones had to be collected by a school bus to travel to a secondary school several kilometres away.

The children then completed their questionnaires with story ideas. These were taken to the computer suite and the children wrote Village Stories directly onto the computer – some collaboratively, others on their own. They were able to use their computing skills, choosing fonts and colours, using WordArt and borders, and importing their own pictures. Lots of discussion and editing on screen took place. The stories were printed and a book made about the village, which was put with the map display for everyone to read.

The next learning opportunity happened in the school hall. The children were able to get into groups and assume a character in the village. They were asked to act out scenes from village life. The children's imagination really brought the village to life.

The children expected that people in the village would want to visit other places and so decided to make leaflets that could go into the post office to advertise local venues. A large variety of leaflets from the library were carefully studied. Armed with this information they all made a leaflet about a visitor attraction of their choice. This, of course, met many literacy targets, but was also a real link to their village.

The children were able to consolidate their research (although this could have acted as a catalyst for the work) by going on a school trip to visit a real village. The village was a few miles outside Chester, situated near the River Dee. It has a large number of Victorian houses so it was decided to focus on that period of architecture, and during the visit time was spent sketching the different designs of houses. The children were made welcome by the vicar who showed them around the church and rang the bells for them. A study of the gravestones showed the age of the church and the children could work out from the dates that many residents had lived only short lives. By reading the names they tried to work out family groups. They also visited the village hall and single shop. As there were the old stocks still in place there was a lively discussion about why people would be punished in the past and placed in the stocks for the day. On the outskirts of the village there were farms with animal stock and smallholdings growing fruit and vegetables.

This study of villages seemed to open endless avenues of study, only some of which were ventured along. There was a real buzz among the children who were able to follow their ideas with meaningful investigation. There was a strong interaction between ideas, research using books, maps and computer resources backed up by a purposeful, well-informed visit. If we need official justification for such work it is provided in the National Curriculum (DfEE/QCA 1999: 11):

> By providing rich and varied contexts for pupils to acquire, develop and apply a
> broad range of knowledge, understanding and skills, the curriculum should enable
> pupils to think creatively and critically. To solve problems and to make a difference

for the better. It should give them the opportunity to become creative, innovative, enterprising and capable of leadership to equip them for future lives as workers and citizens.

History

Most starting points for the delivery of history, because of the National Curriculum, begin with coverage, but are these the best kinds of starting point? History is a subject that all pupils can engage with creatively through simple steps. Children have the opportunity to ask the question 'How does this differ from my experience of life?' about any period of history. This one simple question can open so many doors for a creative approach to the study of history. By resisting the view that history can only be thought about in set periods of time the child has the opportunity to compare, to contrast, to discuss and to invest themselves in the study.

A series of Ofsted reports into the teaching of history have acknowledged that while there is evidence of improvement it remains an area where there is a significant amount of poor teaching and where some cross-curricular approaches (ironically) have worked *against* the nature of historical study. A clear example of this is evidenced in the way that what purports to be historical enquiry actually turns out to be exercises in English: half a dozen statements about the Greeks become not so much a chronological ordering exercise as one in grammatical and narrative structure. Ideally, it is the *business* of history that needs to be addressed, nurtured and encouraged, and this offers the teacher enormous potential.

Chronology and narrative combine in English and historical work in a more productive way. Any historical study needs a scene-setting, just like a novel. Pupils need to know about people (characters), they need to know about the geography of the time (scene setting) and they need to have some intimate knowledge about the 'personality', 'flavour' and 'location' of the period in much the same way that we need to know about motivation, plot and development in the openings of a novel. Historical novels are a good way into this process and I've used passages from Leon Garfield's *Smith* to look at Victorian Britain, and *The Devil's Mill* and *Whistling Clough* by Walt Unsworth during a comparative study of Derbyshire. Beyond this, though, the teacher can use a wealth of locally published materials typically available through local post offices and libraries. Among those I have used in the past have been:

- *Tales from the Mines* by Geoffrey Carr;
- *Ghosts and Legends of the Peak District* by David Clarke; and
- *Haunted Cheshire* by Tom Slemen.

One of the joys of these publications is that they immediately open themselves up for creative interpretations and responses. Take, for example, the story of the Harecastle Boggart. Harecastle is the name of a canal tunnel at Kidsgrove and a Boggart is a local name for a ghost in Staffordshire (the story is easily located in an internet search). A ghost story set in Victorian times can be a memorable experience. Visits to the actual site become fascinating adventures offering a range of opportunities to raise the issue of distinguishing between historical fact and fiction. One of the joys of starting with such a fiction is that these stories regularly use documented evidence to support their 'authenticity', allowing for considerable debate and discussion. More than once I have arranged for children on a site visit to meet a passer-by who has his/her own version of events to tell, or who has new evidence to offer about a particular sighting.

Case study

A teacher that Russell worked with had a policy of opening up the study of history for children to explore avenues of both individual and group interest in a most creative way. Christine's school planned (as many do) to cover the history curriculum by allocating units to different year groups, and this teacher covered the Roman (and Celtic) Britain unit with her mixed Year 4 and Year 5 class. Christine organised her curriculum so that there were two strands to the coverage. In the first strand she located all the key concepts and skills that she wanted all the class to cover. This included work on:

- a broad look at Celtic Britain;
- the Roman invasion;
- the Roman army; and
- roads, maps and places.

Lessons were designed and delivered to cover the National Curriculum history requirements related to chronological understanding, knowledge and understanding of events, and changes in the past and historical enquiry. Christine's second strand employed very different approaches. Once the pupils had an understanding of Roman life in Britain they were asked to begin to develop a specific individual or group interest in a particular area. Pupils selected ideas such as:

- food;
- law and punishment;
- animals in Roman times; and
- clothing.

Of course, this created opportunities for ownership within the historical study selected, but Christine's intentions ran much deeper than this.

Russell: There have always been opportunities in primary schools for children to develop particular interests, why did you decide that history was the best place for this to happen in your classroom?

Christine: Well, to be honest, I think that there aren't that many opportunities for children to make real choices about their interests and their learning these days and you have to work at creating these opportunities now. It's far too easy to let whole-class instruction become the norm, when instead it is more interesting and actually more valuable for children to investigate personal interests. History just seems so full of potential . . .

Russell: But how do you then monitor progress at an individual level? Doesn't it get chaotic?

Christine: Quite the opposite really. I use these opportunities to achieve all kinds of ends. If I know there is a group that really need to start using information technology to a greater degree then I guide them towards using computer resources to aid them with their research. If there are those who are demonstrating a real interest for design and technology, I might use the opportunity to expand and stretch their abilities by, say, designing and building a Roman fort to the specifications and layout they have discovered.

If we look at the experience of two pupils moving through this process it begins to illustrate the creative potential for the subject. Joanne and Rebecca were unsure about their area of interest and had spent some time in the school library looking at possibilities. While they were there they went through one of the cupboards and came across an ancient teaching resource pack. The text was outdated, the illustrations were poor and the whole package had been abandoned for some time. Having looked through the various workcards they selected one and presented their teacher with a suggestion. The card had an illustration of a makeshift stove that was typical of those built by Roman soldiers sent to guard Hadrian's Wall. The text was dense and the illustration was crude but there was a full recipe for 'Spicy Cabbage Soup'. Their suggestion was that they built a working replica of the stove in the grounds of the school and cooked an 'authentic' Roman meal for the rest of the class.

The teacher thought that idea was potentially worthwhile but was dubious about how many class members would be interested in eating spicy cabbage soup. Then she read the recipe. The two girls had clearly suggested the idea having seen that many recipes used by Roman soldiers stationed in the cold included wine in the cooking. Predictably, the recipe for spicy cabbage soup included this ingredient!

Christine agreed, provided the necessary ingredients and surreptitiously included a bottle of non-alcoholic wine. Midday assistants volunteered to help with food preparation and the head teacher agreed to oversee the project. It was interesting to see the results of this project; not only did the pupils achieve their ends, they wrote and delivered a presentation on the subject of 'Food in Roman Britain' to introduce their prepared meal which was eaten with broken bread (and great gusto once the remaining class members discovered that 'wine' was part of the deal!). It was interesting that the two girls developed this interest into an investigation into pottery, eating utensils and design patterns of the times. Together, they made a final creative act: a 'Roman' bowl that was elaborately decorated with a Celtic knot design (Figure 5.1).

When it was pointed out to them that this artefact would never have existed and that the two sides had, in fact, been in conflict, their response was that they had studied Romans and Celtic Britain at the same time, that the bowl was not meant to be authentic (in the way that the meal had been), but that they wanted to create something that brought the two sides of the study together in order to complete their investigation.

The National Curriculum's requirements for organisation and communication were used in a particularly creative way. Instead of the more traditional forms of writing, these children not only developed their findings as part of presentations to other class members but some also took this another stage further, into peer-tutoring.

Figure 5.1

Russell: What brought about the idea of peer-tutoring?

Christine: I came across the idea when I was studying for my Master's degree and used it as the subject of a library retrieval exercise. Afterwards it set me thinking about the potential it could have. I planned a peer-tutoring session a couple of months later and the children were thrilled by it – there were none of the behavioural problems I had imagined; they just thought it was a brilliant thing to do.

Russell: So how did it evolve into what we've seen here?

Christine: What I did was sell it to the children at the beginning of the school year. By then word had got round that in my class some children got the chance to 'do a lesson'. What I suggested was that over the course of the year everyone would get the same chance – in a group of three this meant perhaps ten peer-tutored sessions, about one a month.

Russell: And the children took to this straight away?

Christine: Well it was a case of once they had seen it happen then they wanted to do it too. The really interesting thing for me was firstly that they quickly realised that they all needed to respond very positively to each other, and then they worked really hard to come up with interesting and original lessons. Some have involved information technology, some involved worksheets, some involved drama! Of course, I was always there to act as a support and a guide, but the initial ideas were always the children's, and I felt my input was to help them develop those ideas into 'real' lessons.

Peer-tutoring is an educational area which has been overlooked in the shift towards whole-class, transmission models of teaching.

The evidence throughout this chapter again suggests that these teachers and pupils were both learning in a creative context. The teachers were clearly aware of their own skills and abilities and were acutely aware of the need to meet the specific requirements of the National Curriculum, but this did not restrict opportunities for their classrooms to become creative places. On the contrary, the teachers in question used genuinely creative approaches to studies within the humanities in order to respond to children's ideas positively and to give them a real stake in the planning and development of their own work.

The case studies show how important it is to capture, nurture and maintain children's interests in the humanities, and this is not likely to be achieved through repetitive and mechanical tasks. It is interesting to see that Ofsted reports are readily acknowledging the ways in which work in the humanities often demonstrates the creative focus of the school. Harrison (2002), for example, recognises and celebrates children's achievements in the humanities. Praise is, however, sometimes restricted to those lessons that simply 'met' the teacher's own objectives, or given to a lesson *because* it supported other work being taught in literacy and numeracy. Of course, it is a good idea to contextualise learning as widely as possible, but a genuinely creative approach to the humanities should not need to be excused or justified; sometimes children need to work outside that week's formal literacy and numeracy objectives and sometimes their own ideas and the quality of the outcomes are all the richer because they had different starting points, different avenues of interest and made different decisions. Sometimes good humanities teaching is not about how closely a lesson plan was followed or about how well lesson objectives were met; it is about how rich was the response by the pupils and how much potential was generated. The good teacher in this context learns to listen as well as talk. The teacher's role here is not negative, neither is it absent – it is a *different* role, one which encourages, facilitates and supports.

Creative touches

- **Storyseeds** (See *Storyseeds: Creating Curriculum Stories* by Fiona Collins, in G. C. Hodges, M. J. Drummond and M. Styles (eds) (2000) *Tales, Tellers and Texts*, London: Cassell.) Strong ideas to connect children to (and empathise with) the past by developing traditional storytelling skills using historical evidence as starting points.

- **Anthologies** If, for example, you are looking at Britain since 1930, ask pupils to get elderly relatives to pass on an anecdote or a memory from their school days. Collect these with photocopies of school photographs. Ensure everything is anonymous and collect the accounts in an anthology.

- **Artefacts** There is a historical dimension to everything you do. Simply by encouraging children to help collect half a dozen items that serve the same purpose, the creative possibilities open up for observational artwork, close descriptive writing, measurement etc. Good starting points would be cameras, irons, shoes, writing tools etc.

- **Local history groups** There are always history groups that can be located through your local library, and there are invariably members who are willing to be 'interviewed' by children. This can be a creative starting point for evidence gathering, interviewing in character, hot-seating etc.

- **Local publications** Every area has its own stories and these are regularly collected and self-published by local enthusiasts. These stories provide wonderful starting points for finding out about the past (particularly when they are just that little bit frightening or involve romance!). Try to locate the author to see if he or she would come into school.

- **Building into drama** To explain the development of settlements choose four 'farmers'. Each grows something different. They meet to exchange goods at a river crossing point – build a bridge – the children move from the audience to perform different activities in the growing town.

- **Oracy** On large sheets of paper some groups draw features of an unpolluted town/island; other groups draw polluted ones. Children present ideas to class for discussion.

- **Technology** Rather than stopping at the consideration of the design and production processes, focus on the business aspects of manufacture. These could include the need for profit; the cost, source and quality of materials; the weight of each item; packaging and transport costs; the shape for ease of storage; sales outlets; attractiveness, presentation and the need to be new.

- **Simple resources** Glue a food-packaging label in the centre of a large sheet of paper. Ask the children to record by labelling what information is given on the food label. This will range from information about nutrition to design details for advertising, country of origin and packaging. Each can be an avenue for further interest as decided by the child.

- **Individual folders of individual research on humanities topics** These should follow a given format with a title page, contents, synopsis, own research, internet page printed, bibliography, appendix, glossary of terms, index. The folders can then be developed as personal interests at home, as part of class extension activities or as a focus for wet playtimes etc.

- Give each child a map of the school field with the outline of the school building on a clipboard. Take the children outside – show them how to orientate the map. The child can then record his/her own details around the school focusing on what is important to their daily lives.

- Use a story/poetry book with a particular location to be a starting point for a cross-curricular investigation. For example, Alan Garner's *Weirdstone of Brisingamen* is a perfect opportunity to locate children's lives at a particular time in history and a particular place geographically.

- Encourage pupils to explore dance as an opportunity to deepen understanding of processes. River stages – fast and active, strong and steady, meandering and slow, dissipating and spreading.

- Use atlases of Britain to find towns on the railway network. Use the internet to plan rail journeys with different objectives – no changes, a long scenic route etc. (www.nationalrail.co.uk).

References

Bage, G. (2000) *Thinking History 4–14*. London: Falmer.

Collins, F. (2000) 'Storyseeds: Creating Curriculum Stories', in Hodges, G. C., Drummond, M. J. and Styles, M. (eds) *Tales, Tellers and Texts*. London: Cassell.

Department for Education and Employment (DfEE/QCA) (1999) *The National Curriculum: Handbook for Primary Teachers in England*. London: DfEE/QCA.

Foley, M. and Janikoun, J. (1996) *The Really Practical Guide to Primary Geography* (2nd edn). Cheltenham: Stanley Thornes.

Harrison, S. (2002) 'Celebrating good practice: identifying features of effective teaching and learning in history'. *Primary History*, April, 15–17.

Qualifications and Curriculum Authority (QCA) (2003) *National Curriculum in Action*. Retrieved 7 November from www.ncaction.org.uk.

Rawling, E. and Westaway, J. (2003) 'Exploring creativity – QCA Creativity Project'. *Primary Geographer*, January, 7–9.

CHAPTER 6

The Performing Arts

John Airs, Jill Wright, Linda Williams and Ruth Adkins

Drama is playing. It is a process (playing) which might ultimately lead to a product (a play), but not necessarily. Art is about playing. Picasso talked about all children being artists, and the problem that most would not be once they grew up. Many of us forget how to play in this way or education takes it away from us. For children, dramatic play is their first art form. It is how they initially engage with life and learning. So drama is, at its simplest, play; but play with a purpose. And that purpose is to make things visible.

A group of girls creates an image as part of a drama about their school culture. They show three girls clearly mocking a fourth who appears to be eating. All the other boys and girls immediately recognise the situation.

'They're laughing at her because she's finishing her school dinner.'

There are four teachers in the room – two class teachers and two advisory drama teachers. None of us understands.

'Oh, don't you know? In this school if you finish your dinner it must be because you're a scav, or you're too poor to eat properly at home so you have to eat everything at school.'

So no-one finishes their dinner. All four teachers are suitably aghast.

'But wait a minute. How many of you would like to finish your dinners?'

All 40 of them put up their hands. Suddenly something has been made visible. Two classes of youngsters realise that they have all been adhering to a code that none of them wants. They have learnt something quite important and they have an opportunity to change things. And it is not just that they have learnt that they are all unhappy with this particular example of an unwanted code; they are now in a position to understand that codes of behaviour in general are not immutable, natural or God-given. They have the power to change at least some things if they can agree that they want to.

So drama is playing – experimenting with images and actions and dialogue in order to make things visible and audible so that some of us can learn things that matter to us. Emile Zola (1866) said of his work in *Mes Haine*: 'If you ask me what I came to do in this world, I, an artist, I will answer you: I am here to live out loud' (Tripp 1976: 39).

Drama is one way of living out loud. We have a forum within which we can say things, hear what we say and hear what others say in reply, and none of it can be charged against us because we were only playing. If it makes sense and others recognise what we are saying, and say 'Yes, me too', then we can admit we meant it. The drama has worked. We have learnt something through the art form and there is a potential for change. And, most importantly, we have had the freedom to experiment safely because it is only a game. There are no right or wrong answers to intimidate us. There are rules, but they are the necessary rules of our game, so that's all right. In the safety of the game we can take risks and perhaps learn unexpected truths. We are free to take risks. We are not playing safe but playing safely.

Theatre

Let us look now a little more closely at the sort of learning we are talking about here and why it might be significant learning. Augusto Boal, who has had some influence on current educational theatre and drama practice, says:

> This is theatre – the art of looking at ourselves . . . Theatre should be happiness. It should help us learn about ourselves and our times. We should know the world we live in, the better to change it . . . Theatre is a form of knowledge; it should and can also be a means of transforming society. Theatre can help us build our future rather than just waiting for it.
>
> (Boal 1992: xxx)

There are three key ideas in this statement: the idea of theatre as happiness; the idea of learning about ourselves and our times; and the idea of transforming our society. Let's look at each in turn.

Theatre and happiness

Drama and theatre in education are fun. They may deal with very serious matters and they may engage our pity and our anger but they must grip us; they must, as even serious old Bertholt Brecht insisted, entertain us. In his poem 'On Judging' (Brecht 1986) addressed to theatre artists (actors, playwrights, directors) he says:

> Let this learning be pleasurable. Learning must be taught
> As an art, and you should

Teach dealing with things and with people
As an art too, and the practice of art is pleasurable.

Educational drama and theatre are serious pleasurable activities. We play the game with commitment and with joy. Theatre should be happiness.

'Are we doing drama?' Children's enthusiasm should be enough to alert us to the significance of this medium for learning. When a teacher sees the impact that the art form can have on even their most reluctant learners any doubts about finding time for yet another activity in the impossibly overcrowded school day can be dispelled. 'They were still talking about it two years later,' a primary head teacher told us, referring to some classroom drama we had been involved in with her pupils several years before. Drama can be happiness and because of that it can stay with us.

Learning about ourselves

'Learning about ourselves and our times' covers quite a wide curriculum. In a sense it covers the whole curriculum. We can even include rather unlikely subjects such as science and maths if we want to. 'That was just like being a real scientist!' a ten-year-old girl said after a science fiction drama in which she had had to analyse evidence, make hypotheses, test them and draw conclusions in collaboration with her classmates. The stimulus was a teacher in role as a mysterious being from another planet. One primary teacher taught her entire maths syllabus for a year with her class in role as high street bankers and customers, business and private, engaged in a series of ventures and tasks (for a fuller account of this project see Ball and Airs 1995). What drama offers us towards learning about ourselves and our times is a context which can be as historically, culturally and politically specific as we wish to make it: as real or as fanciful; as naturalistic or as stylised; as reassuring or as challenging. It can make visible the roots, the causes, the implications and the effects of our actions. It can involve us deeply and engage us critically. We can learn about ourselves and our times, across the whole curriculum.

Transforming society

So far, so good. There is nothing particularly contentious or surprising in all this. But what about Boal's third claim that 'Drama is potentially a means of transforming our society'? That is quite a claim. Is it valid? And if it is, are we as teachers up to it? Are we willing or indeed entitled to take on what sounds like such an overtly political task?

Perhaps it would be less threatening – and more accurate – to say that drama is a means of allowing us to see what we might need to change, why we might need to change it and possibly even how we might go about changing it. This is not to argue that all drama in education must be a form of *agit prop* theatre, though some might be, but it is to acknowledge that all representations of how we live are, without exception, political, in the sense that the relationships they depict are politically determined. The image of society reflected in the drama cannot be other than a political one. The structures and hierarchies and power plays, the interests being served, the voices being ignored or dismissed, are all there (even the absent voices), whether we remark on them or not. And, of course, the most political strategy of all political strategies is to pretend they are not there at all – 'The world is the way it is and there's nothing anyone can do about it'. Drama can help us to see that there are some things we might want to change and there are some things we can try to change if we are actually conscious that they are there. For example, we could all agree to fight the idea that there *must* be very poor and very wealthy people in society, or we could all agree to finish our school dinners – if we wanted to.

Perhaps we might realise that the grossly expensive trainers we are destroying our family's happiness to acquire are not only an essential mark of how cool we are – without them life would be simply unendurable – but that they are also our generous contribution to the millionaire lifestyles of the principal Nike shareholders. If we realise that by following the crowd we are all acting as the shareholders' stooges, and effectively mugging ourselves, we might be in a position to change it.

How could drama reveal this? Well, perhaps by presenting the domestic mayhem that buying trainers may cause. Then, in role as Nike's marketing managers, we could explore what we imagine their planning strategy must be. How do they get us to serve their interests so enthusiastically?

> 'I have it, MD! How about if we get the kids to do the marketing for us? Make them ashamed to be seen dead in anything worth less than £90 a pair. Think of it as infant power dressing!'

And if anyone thinks we are being unfair to multinational companies we can invite a representative in to tell us what it's really like. They might even give us each a pair of Air Max IIs to keep us quiet!

But what if some of us like things the way they are? What if we don't want to give up power dressing even if we can see it for the dastardly capitalist ploy that it is. We like Air Max IIs and Dad would only spend the money he saved on booze anyway. We're doing them all a favour really! And think of all those Nike workers. They need our custom to keep them in work. One of the many telling things that Peter Brook has to say about theatre is relevant here: 'Theatre has the potential – unknown in other art forms – of replacing a single viewpoint by a multitude of different visions' (Brook 1988: 15).

A novelist may imagine a multitude of different voices: the participants in a drama will both imagine them and realise them from within their own genuine differences. Even if they are actors performing someone else's text they will bring to that text their own visions of the world and the dialogue is then not only between characters but between the author and the actors (as well as the director and the designer and the audiences). If the drama is a classroom drama, created by students and teacher and subject to every nuance of individual and collective insight they offer, then the dialogue will incorporate as many divergent views as are present within the group. That is if the structure and management of the play are effective in letting all the voices be heard – and not all at once! Although drama may expose what some of us uncritically regard as 'truths', as a method of indoctrination it is not particularly effective. It cannot force anyone to accept ideas. In fact, one of the unique virtues of drama as a learning medium is its potential for allowing more than one voice to be heard. It is potentially the most democratic medium, and educational drama can be its most democratic form.

Having made something present so that we can publicly recognise it, and having tried out our own possibly conflicting stances, how do we move on from here to transform society? Well, of course, drama does not transform society and Boal wasn't claiming that it does. But it can be a *means* of transforming it. Writing about the Elizabethan and Jacobean theatre, Franco Moretti (1983: 42) considers that 'Having deconsecrated the king, tragedy made it possible to decapitate him'. We are not suggesting that classroom drama should make it possible to behead a second Charles, but it can make invisible forces and structures and interests visible, so that our students may have some possibility of controlling them. This could be the first step towards building a future rather than just waiting for it.

Structures of feeling

Once we have discovered that because something happens all the time that does not mean that it is natural or inevitable, then we may be in a position to change things. Understanding this involves a singular sort of learning. It represents a shift in what Raymond Williams (1977: 121) calls our 'structures of feeling'. There is a sort of knowing that we might call 'knowing in the head'. Much, if not most, of what we were formally taught in school led to that kind of knowing. Some of it has been useful though most has been long-forgotten. But we also learn in ways that go far deeper than that. We can acquire understanding that shapes our perception, knowledge that is significant to the way we live, to the way we are, knowledge that affects our structures of feeling. In schools, much of this sort of knowledge is acquired through what we sometimes call the hidden curriculum and we spend the rest of our lives trying to unlearn it. Imagine if we could put this sort of knowledge onto the curriculum and deal with it honestly and critically. Theatre and drama in education aspire to providing this sort of knowledge. The following response from a Wigan pupil to one of the last productions of the sadly deceased theatre-in-education company Pit Prop testifies to how far this claim may be justified:

> The production I saw yesterday meant a lot to me. Before I went into the hall to see the production I did not like black people but when I came out of the hall from the first half I had changed my mind a little but when I came back it really hit me. What was really happening.
>
> Ian asked us to read what was wrote. It really made me sick what white people were calling black people, and when I came out of the production I was shaking with rage because I think it is so horrible. I just can't write enough to describe how much your production has made me think and question myself like have I ever told any jokes and made fun of black people.

This boy certainly learned something. This is 'felt knowledge' he is describing, felt in his whole body. He was shaking with rage. More than this, he is already referring his new understanding to his own behaviour, to his own life. He is beginning to question a whole set of social values. He has had a significant experience and has been helped to reflect on it. He would appear to be creating new structures of feeling for himself. He may go on to look for ways to change the social structures that produced the situations which so incensed him. He may look for those through drama and in real life.

Clearly, drama does not work as powerfully as this on every occasion, but there are several identifiable components in effective drama which might explain how it works. First, there is the representation of a recognisable human situation – particular, idiosyncratic, perhaps funny, surprising, touching, alarming – but believable. Second, this situation is presented so that it resonates beyond the particular to the point where all involved realise that they are involved – we are intrigued, enlightened, reassured, taken by surprise, disturbed; whatever it is, it matters, it connects. This can happen whether the drama is presented by others or created by ourselves. However, it is most effective if we are actively involved.

This leads us to the third component. When an actress, on hearing a student in the discussion after the play advise that the troubled, truanting character she has been playing should try talking to her mum, suddenly responds indignantly in role, 'Why should I talk to her? She doesn't care!', all the significance of her frustration and confusion is felt by the whole audience. There is surprised laughter but there is also a thrill of excitement and expectation as this new moment of drama is opened up. A new game is on. It is now more than a discussion, because anything might happen, and that 'anything' will be realised as fully rounded human behaviour. It will be emotionally and intuitively fleshed out, and anyone can join in! The energy level and enthusiasm of the group is immediately engaged several gears higher than before. Serious learning is about to take place. One girl argues with the actress, trying to convince her she should talk to her mum. The actress, still in role as Kelly, is not persuaded. 'Come and show us what Kelly might say, then,' says the theatre company's facilitator. The fourteen-year-old girl is prevailed on to come all the way from the back and faces Kelly's mum, another actress, on stage. She is now Kelly, and forcefully insists that her mum stop evading key issues that are driving them apart. Mum does not accede easily but Kelly pursues her with determination. It is good theatre and it is good education. The young audience analyses the situation keenly and with some fervour. A boy volunteers to play Kelly and earns a round of applause for his artful approach to the problem. In private conversation, afterwards, the girl who took over Kelly's role said she'd learnt a lot: she was always having rows with her mum; this whole experience had afforded her a new perspective on their relationship. (These examples were originally published in *Theatre in Education: Performing for You*, a North West Arts Board Information Pack written by John Airs 1994.)

Open learning

The fourth component of effective drama is to do with the openness of this sort of learning. There is a significant order of knowing and understanding which must be seen as a process, which can never be complete. There is no finished product. There is an ambivalence, uncertainty and a suggestiveness about this learning. It is the sort of knowing and understanding over which we argue, over which we may disagree, over which we can change our thinking. It is the sort of knowing and understanding by which we live our complicated and confusing lives. To say that this sort of knowing can never be complete is not to say that everything is relative, that there is no truth; it is simply to say that our understanding, our knowledge of the truth, is necessarily always on the move.

The process is a dialectical one. In order to know or understand something of any measure of complexity, we must form a thesis which, however brilliant we are, will always carry within it at least one contradiction or omission. The seed of this contradiction or incompleteness will grow, if we acknowledge it, until we have formed an antithesis. If we wish to retain what is left of the truth of our original thesis while recognising the contradictory truth of the emerging under-standing, the antithesis, then we must resolve the developing thinking into a synthesis. The synthesis becomes our new thesis, our new understanding, which in turn will carry its own contradictions and deficiencies, and these in turn, if we see them and acknowledge them, will lead to a new antithesis, and so on, for ever. One of the characters in Tom Stoppard's play *Jumpers* says: 'The truth is always an interim judgment'.

'But there must have been some decent Romans!' argued a teacher in the early stages of a drama about the Roman occupation of Lincoln. We were all teachers on a drama course in Lincoln. The young teacher, in role as the commanding officer of the garrison, spent the next hour or so attempting to prove that that might be true. He set out to be a benevolent imperialist. At first he seemed to be doing quite well, conceding this to one interest group, yielding that to another, until, in the face of sullen Celtic resistance, recalcitrant Roman artisans, awkward legionnaires and a ferocious wife who had far firmer ideas about how to do his job than he had, he gradually negotiated, wheedled and blustered his way to a complete standstill. He literally stopped in the middle of the drama, at a fairly climactic moment, and said, 'I'm sorry, I just don't know what to do!'

In the discussion that followed nobody came up with any solution that might remotely have worked, other than divorce and a request for home leave. In the bar, after the session, the young teacher confessed privately how awful he felt because he'd let everyone down and ruined the drama. It took some persuading to get him to realise that he'd been responsible for a wonderful piece of drama. He had exposed perfectly the contradiction implicit in the thesis that you could be a benevolent imperialist and succeed in satisfying everyone. His personal embarrassment prevented him from seeing what the rest of us saw, which, if he'd managed to contain it within the fiction, by taking hemlock or something, would have concluded the drama brilliantly. As it was, the learning point had been made, even if not dramatically resolved to his satisfaction.

So, what is the nature of the learning that may take place in drama and theatre in education? It is a learning through play, which allows us to take risks with how we see ourselves and our society. It is about making things visible in order, ultimately, to expose the contradictions which might lead to a new understanding, a new knowing, of the complex sort that Brecht was after when he talked of 'complex seeing' in the theatre. And this knowing is more than a mere 'knowing in the head', it is a knowing which affects our very structures of feeling. Williams (1981: 147–8) suggested, 'It is clear that certain forms of social relationships are deeply embedded in certain forms of art'. And 'it was above all in drama that the processes of change in conception of the self and society were articulated and realised'.

We have presented a range of drama theories with examples of practice to illustrate them. But what happens when you take some of these ideas through a series of lessons? The following example shows how one teacher turned some of these theories into practice.

Studying war through drama

One of the most challenging subjects on the primary curriculum must be the subject of war. The contradictions and complexities within a child's feelings about war present us with an educational minefield. Direct experience of war is a reality most of us in mainland Britain may have escaped, but it is a reality that in another sense we cannot escape. Responsibility for war (as a nation), news of war and, since September 2001, fear of war may weigh on us, may haunt our dreams and the dreams of our children. Could we help those children to take a look at this reality through the protective lens of a dramatic fiction?

The following case study describes how Jill Wright used drama, music and dance to explore understanding of World War II. The series of lessons was planned to complement other work that the Year 6 class were doing about the Second World War. It was felt that the children needed to deepen their understanding of the period, the impact of war on the people and relate this to the world today.

Lesson 1: air raids

The children were shown photographs of everyday life in the 1940s. These re-inforced the idea that people had to continue their daily activities: shopping, going to school, cleaning windows, etc. during the time of the air strikes. Following discussion, each group role-played a scene from everyday life. Each scene was then held to become a freeze-frame while a recording of an air-raid siren was played.

An eerie silence was followed by the playing of 'The Sinking' from the sound-track of the film *Titanic*. Next, having examined the various shelters (e.g. Morrison, Anderson, underground stations) as part of previous work, the children were able to devise movements accompanied by the music which took them from their everyday lives into the shelters. The children's movements reflected the panic following the siren as people desperately tried to find shelter. They used a variety of movements to reflect this, some searching for family members who were not with them at the time, others dragging people to safety. As one child said, 'I felt really scared when that siren went off'.

The children were encouraged to create freeze-frames of what it was like in the shelters. Some chose to cower and protect each other, others chose to make part of the group into the actual shelter, while others took refuge inside. There was then an opportunity for the children to use thought-tracking to shout out their thoughts about being in the shelter. It soon became apparent, through assessment of the children's responses, that they had deepened their under-standing of the severity and scale of the situation. Cries of 'Where's our John? I hope he's safe!' 'I'm scared Mummy!' 'What if we can't get out?' 'What if our house gets bombed?', among others, were heard across the hall.

Meanwhile, a group of children had been working on creating music to depict the actual air raid. They chose instruments which they thought would reflect the sounds made by the aircraft and the bombs. They decided to make the music tell the 'story' of the air raid (programmatic music) with a crescendo as the planes approached, a climax as the bombs dropped and a diminuendo as the planes left once their mission was accomplished. They achieved this not only through dynamics but also through combinations of instruments. The children were able to create a graphic music score (Figure 6.1) due to previous lessons which had introduced this concept.

The air raid can be seen clearly in the score. The plastic tube serves as the warning, the zither and bells act as the drone of the approaching aircraft, the wood blocks enter as the sound intensifies. The drums playing two sounds to each one of the bells represent gunfire, while the cymbal sounded the dropping of the bombs. After the crescendo of noise, repeated over two bars, the sequence is played in reverse as the planes leave the scene. The children then incorporated this musical sequence into the drama by playing it as the rest of the class were in position in the air-raid shelters.

The scene was broken to examine photographic evidence of the results of the bombing. Each group was given a photograph on a large piece of paper and the children then worked together to write words on the paper to describe the scene and the feelings of people looking at the scene. After discussing their ideas with the rest of the class the children went back to their positions they had held at

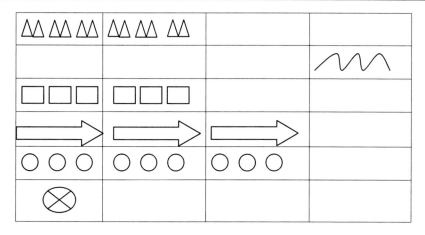

Figure 6.1 Children's graphic music score

the end of the air raid. The music for 'Death of Ase' from Grieg's *Peer Gynt Suite* was played as the children emerged from the shelters to examine the damage inflicted on their homes and the surrounding area by the air attack. The music creates a sombre mood and the children were encouraged to create their own movements as they emerged from the shelter to reflect the horrors which they saw before them. Finally, freeze-frame was used to hold the movements and expressions to end the session.

Lesson 2: evacuation

Realising the horror and effects of air raids was fundamental to the understanding of why children were evacuated during the Second World War. For that reason, lesson two explored the thoughts and feelings of families involved in evacuation.

A suitcase containing objects which may have been packed by an evacuee in 1939 was shown to the children. The kinds of objects included clothes, a Bible, dominoes and other old toys, a book, etc. This led to a discussion about what the children would take with them today if they were evacuated, and included reflections on modern conflicts such as Kosovo. In a subsequent lesson the children made two suitcases out of paper, one based in 1939, the other from a modern-day evacuee.

In groups of four or five, the children improvised a scene at home the night before they were evacuated. No guidance was given to the children on who should be in the scene, but many chose to have absent fathers (on active service), grandparents and children between the ages of 5 and 14, as others would have been evacuated. This served as a useful assessment point because it showed that the children had understood the difficulties faced by many families at this time. The children were asked to improvise some dialogue and show the scene to the rest of the class. Many magical moments occurred as it became clear from watching these scenes that the children's historical understanding had been greatly extended through the use of drama techniques: they were 'living history'.

Mother:	Make sure that you behave and are polite with who you are billeted with. I don't want people thinking that we don't know how to bring up our children in the city.
Child 1:	But mum, I don't want to go. It's not fair! Why doesn't she have to go?
Mother:	Because she's only 4 and she has to stay with me.
Child 2:	I can't wait to go! It'll be great. We've never been on a train and I've heard there's lots of food in the country.
Child 1 (crying):	But I'll miss mum and grandma, and what if dad gets back while we're away?
Mother:	(also close to tears) Then we'll come and visit you. Now you'd better go and pack, and don't forget to put in your Bible.
Child 2:	Come on, don't be such a wimp. I'll look after you.

After watching these scenes the action transferred to the railway station. Keeping in the family group the children used movement to express their feelings on saying goodbye to their families. Music was not used at this point because although music can dictate a general mood, the moods reflected by the children's movements were necessarily diverse. Some skipped and jumped onto the train showing the excitement of a new adventure, whereas others moved slowly and deliberately to reflect the conflicting emotion of sadness and trepidation.

Later, music was introduced using spoken chants. Each group wrote down a thought that the children might have had on the train journey:

'What an adventure'

'I don't want to go'

'I miss my Mum'

'Who will I stay with?'

'I'm running away'.

Each group repeated a chant to reflect the gathering sound and speed of the train and echoing the conflicting feelings of the children on board. After reaching a crescendo, each group stopped speaking until only one group's chant was left and the journey had effectively ended.

Lesson 3: billeting

This lesson began with the music of 'Morning' from Grieg's *Peer Gynt*. The children used stretching/awakening movements to reflect getting off a train after a long journey. The teacher acted in role as the billeting officer, marshalling the children into lines and taking them to the village/school hall. The children were divided into evacuees and hosts and the selection scene role-played. This, again, produced the opportunity to assess the children's understanding of the situation as the diversity of experience was represented through the dialogue. Some families were split as only girls or boys would be taken, not both. Some hosts appeared kind, while others simply appeared to be looking for workers.

Following the selection scene the children were divided into groups of three or four and introduced to a range of evidence about billeting and the experiences of evacuees. This included oral evidence, photographs, newspaper reports and letters. Each group was given an experience that the evacuees might have had, e.g. life on a farm, working in a house, playing in the countryside, fishing, haymaking etc. Children either worked simultaneously on the same action – for example casting a line and catching a fish – or in a complementary way, e.g. one person hooking the line, another casting and a third hauling in the fish. A very different experience was reflected by a group who chose to have two children cleaning out the cowsheds followed by a sudden beating from the host. The children then reeled and circled away ending crumpled and still on the floor.

Dear Mum,

I am having a great time here in Maeshafn. The people that I have been billeted with are very kind to me. They let me call them Auntie Pat and Uncle Frank. They don't have any children of their own, but I have made lots of new friends anyway.

Every Tuesday Auntie Pat takes me to visit her sister who lives in Mold and she gives me biscuits which she makes herself. They are delicious! Uncle Frank lets me help look after the vegetables in the garden and on Sundays, when Auntie Pat goes to church, I help Uncle Frank wash his truck until it shines.

School is great now. At first, people called me names and pushed me around because I spoke differently, but after a while we all started to play football together. My best friend is called David and we go fishing together.

I hope that you are well. It would be great if you could come and visit. Auntie Pat and Uncle Frank can't wait to meet you. Say hello to Dad for me.

Lots of love, Peter

Dear Mum,

It's me, Elsie. I hate it here in Llandudno. Please let me come home to you. I don't care about the bombs, I just need to get away from this terrible place.

The family I am billeted with are called the Johnsons. At first, I thought it was going to be great because they live in a big posh house with a big garden, but I soon realised that they just wanted me to be a servant. The other servants have gone away to war or to work in the factories and Mrs Johnson says that I must work to earn my keep.

I have to get up at 5.30 a.m. and make the breakfast, but I'm not allowed to eat with the family in the dining room, I have to eat on my own in the kitchen. Then I have to do all the washing and ironing. If I've finished my chores I go to school in the afternoon.

The Johnsons have two children of their own called Mary and Harriet. I thought that we would be able to play together, but the girls hate me being there. Last week, Harriet wet her bed and blamed me. Mrs Johnson slapped me really hard and then I had to wash all the sheets.

I will try to be a brave girl because I know you think it is safer for me here, but I'm so unhappy. Please come for me.

Your daughter, Elsie

Throughout this work the children thought carefully about their body positions, movements and facial expressions and worked to produce a group scene rather than individual pictures. The children were also asked to comment on the action through thought bubbles.

After this lesson the children were asked to write in role as an evacuee choosing the kind of experience that they wished to reflect. This provided an opportunity to assess how effective the drama had been in developing the children's understanding of the period. The two letters opposite were written by two children and demonstrate the power of this method of teaching.

The children who took part in the lessons and wrote these letters can be seen reading them in role on the BBC Children's History website for Merseyside (bbc.co.uk/schools/4–11 history).

Dance

You will have noticed that the drama included 'choreographed' sequences of movement within the drama. A dance piece in its own right is very different, sometimes intimidating to create, as the idea of movement for its own sake can seem blank and scarily open to any interpretation. In the face of this, dance can become the exaggerated acting out of actions, like stylised mime. Knowing the vocabulary and structure of choreography gives direction to creativity in dance, allowing us to make pieces that are subtle and interesting. Although technique is important at all levels, for safety reasons, children don't need to be brilliant technicians to dance and choreograph in a way that is imaginative and engaging. Simple movements can be very powerful, and simple ideas can sometimes be the best starting points.

Dance vocabulary describes five basic movements that make up most dance – travelling, gesture, jump, turn and stillness. These movements and their variations are combined to form motifs or phrases, and these motifs can be varied or developed and arranged to form a dance. Motif development involves adding dynamics to a phrase to change it and adds a certain tone to a piece. Dynamics deal with time, weight, space and flow. A movement can be slow, heavy, large and smooth, or quick, light, high and jerky, or any combination of adjectives and adverbs to create the feel you want. Structuring of dance works similarly to music, with the most common forms being binary (AB), ternary (introducing new section then returning to original, gives sense of balance and completion, ABA), rondo (verse and chorus, ABACADA), narrative (storytelling, ABCD).

This vocabulary describes who does what, when, where and how. However, dancers can also leave a class or a performance asking 'Why?'. This does not need to be out of the confusion some people feel when wondering what a dance means. As well as giving dancers new experiences of working together creatively, dance can carry a message and make the dancers (or their audience) think. Dancers communicate through their own movement, both movement quality and actual motion, and other elements, such as form or the way movement fits or contrasts with music, can say just as much.

Although some dance pieces are made purely from movement-based (kinaesthetic) stimuli, it is easier to direct energy and ideas with a clear idea of what you are dancing about (although it depends on what the dance is for). A theme studied in other subjects can be a good starting point, because children will already have discussed it, and dancing about it can inspire new ideas and viewpoints.

The *raison d'être* of creative arts subjects is their role as a vehicle to express creative ideas. Although music, dance and drama are also highly motivational for many pupils, they have a hard intellectual edge, just like any other subject. For example, issues of power, equality and critical exploration of truths are particularly important areas for the performing arts. Theories about these issues and the other ideas that we have discussed in the chapter will guide your planning and implementation of drama lessons. At first the children will experience these ideas implicitly, but later in their school career they will begin to explicitly reflect on how these things might affect the lives of themselves and others.

Creative touches

- Expand the meaning of a single theme by brainstorming its associations. For example, from the theme of 'falling', we can draw out falling asleep, falling out, falling down.

- Props – pillows, sponge balls, elastics – particularly used with older dancers who have some dance experience, introduce more relationships to think about within the dance.

- Alphabet – assign a movement or dynamic to each letter of the alphabet (Arch, Bound, Clasp, Drop). Dancers can make phrases out of the letters in their name, or choose another word as stimulus.

- Characters – just as in drama, taking on a well-thought-out character can inspire dancers. Children could create their own computer game characters, with characteristic ways of moving and 'special moves'.

- Chance – think of six separate movements, then number them one to six and throw dice to decide their order. This makes for a less obvious and sometimes surprising sequence of movements.

- Floor patterns – a chain of dancers tracing clear floor patterns with their movement might seem simple but is very effective.

- Simple abstract ideas – conflict, friendship, fear – can inspire movement or dynamics for a piece.

- Finding ways into drama. Sometimes a moment will occur in a lesson when you are discussing or reading something together, and you think, 'I wonder what that would look like. Shall we try it?' Starting a drama can be as simple as that. Volunteers create an image of the moment, or you, the teacher, address the class in role. 'The fire appears to be beyond control. You are his privy councillors. His majesty will want our advice.' It may not be extensive or even well-informed advice but whatever they offer should be taken seriously, clarifications sought for and implications drawn. 'But what will the citizens say when you demand they pull down their houses while the flames are still some streets away?' All that such low-key role play asks of you and the children is that you take it seriously as far as you can. You can always stop and reflect, out of role, on what is happening. Ask their advice on how to handle your role. 'Would the duke be willing to get involved in the fire fighting himself?' In fact, he did, but that historical fact might be disclosed later. If they think it would be beneath your dignity then you can go along with that for the time being. They may be intrigued to discover the truth was otherwise.

- A riveting account of the Fire of London can be found in Neil Hanson's *The Dreadful Judgement* (2001) (London: Corgi). One of the wisest books on how to use role play is *So You Want to Use Role Play?* by Gavin Bolton and Dorothy Heathcote (1999) (Stoke: Trentham Books). It is wise not to attempt too much. Let a drama develop slowly, step by step. Draw up maps and documents; invent or 'research' characters; develop images and investigate them carefully – what might this character be thinking, feeling, going to do next? Never rush things. Always reflect.

- The key questions to ask of any dramatic moment are questions like: Why is this happening? What exactly is happening and what is its significance? What might the consequences be? These questions can be asked out of role or they might suggest the next dramatic activity: 'Can you show us that?' An important task for us as teachers is to help draw out the significance of what the children are showing. The girls who wanted to challenge the 'no-one-finishes-her-dinner-here' rule needed the teacher to ask what the others thought. It was when they all admitted the rule was silly that the moment of recognition was achieved – a dramatic moment but, in a sense, outside of the drama.

- Dramatic activities do not have to involve all-singing, all-dancing performances. They may just be pairs of children talking in role, writing in role or texting or phoning each other in role. These tasks may be fed back to the others as mini-performances or, perhaps more usefully, as brief reports on what transpired.

- Small-group work is often the most productive when the task set is tightly structured. 'Prepare a sequence of three images depicting the events', rather than 'Go off and improvise a scene'. Walking before running is a useful principle. Just making it up as we go along can easily become superficial play unless a clear focus and some element of structure are provided.

- Building a world physically, with crumpled newspaper and cloth or papier-mâché can be a useful way into a drama. Setting the scene, as it were, is often a valuable first task. There are various ways of doing it. We might simply describe it together. We might draw it up on a length of lining paper. We might use our own bodies to create physical objects. A little boy being man-handled over cobbles turned out to be a piano that a group of emigrants were optimistically bringing to their boat.

- A parachute is a handy resource. It can become almost anything, transforming itself from Scheherazade's bed to the storm of dust from which the 40 thieves emerge; from the council table to the Pied Piper's cloak (he rises up through the hole in the middle of the 'table'); from the river to the mountain which swallows up rats and children; from long fields of barley and of rye to the magic web with colours gay on the island of Shalott. It can also be simply a lovely plaything for creative, co-operative play.

- Stories, tales and poems can provide effective stimuli for dramatic explorations. What might happen to Burglar Bill if he goes shoplifting in Mothercare? One half of the class in role as CCTV figures mirror the actions of the other half as Bill and other shoppers, assistants, security guards, police. The Wolf catches sight of the boiling pot in the nick of time and decides to approach the house built of bricks some other way. The children who went on the bear hunt with their dad face their mum who wants to know exactly how their clothes got into this state, and what are these scratches on the front door? The poor sad bear! Shall we visit him in his cave? But this time, we'll plan the expedition properly!

These and many other dramas can be found in the three *Speaking, Listening and Drama* books for teachers by John Airs and Chris Ball (2002) (Leamington Spa: Hopscotch Educational Publishing) and in *Key Ideas, Drama* by the same authors (1997) (Dunstable: Folens).

- In Dorothy Heathcote's *mantle of the expert* dramas the children work as members of an establishment with specific tasks and responsibilities to carry out. This form of drama may last for weeks or even months and will cover many areas of the curriculum. The full account of this approach is presented in *Drama for Learning* by Dorothy Heathcote and Gavin Bolton (1995) (Portsmouth: Heinemann).

References

Ball, C. and Airs, J. (1995) *Taking Time To Act*. Portsmouth, NH: Heinemann.

Boal, A. (1992) *Games for Actors and Non-Actors*. London: Routledge.

Brecht, B. (1986) *Poems 1913–1956*. London: Methuen.

Brook , P. (1988) *The Shifting Point*. London: Methuen.

Moretti, F. (1983) *Signs Taken for Wonders*. London: Verso.

Tripp, R. T. (ed.) (1976) *The International Thesaurus of Quotations*. Hamondsworth: Penguin.

Williams, R. (1977) *Marxism and Literature*, Oxford: Oxford University Press.

Williams, R. (1981) *Culture*. Glasgow: Glasgow: Fontana.

CHAPTER 7

Visual Arts

Ivy Roberts and Helen Hilditch

My two long lives – in education and in art – have left me greatly strengthened in the beliefs that began to dawn on me as a young man. I believe that each one of us is born with creative power – with the attributes of the artist and the craftsman. I believe that the arts must be at the very centre, the core of our lives. I believe that if the proper dignity of every human being were respected and his or her native gifts were well nourished and cherished we should then reach our full stature and come into our rightful heritage – and help others to theirs.

(Tanner 1987: 214)

In this text, the inspector Robin Tanner affirmed the need to place the child at the centre of the learning process and ascribed to the arts a position of vital importance in the creative development of the child. Tanner's words acknowledged the best of primary practice at the time and encouraged teachers to address the needs of individual children.

The potential for addressing the individual needs of children is boundless in art. From the moment children can hold a mark-making tool they enjoy mapping the movements of their hands and arms and will do so enthusiastically on any available surface, as every parent knows. From this they progress to storytelling through increasingly sophisticated scribbles from which patterns of symbols or schema start to emerge. Through these, young children make sense of their surroundings and begin to convey meaning. Imagine a 5–6-year-old's drawing of a house to conjure up an immediate mind's eye picture of the symbols used to depict roof, door, windows, sun, etc.

In engaging with simple materials, such as crayons, pencil and paper, children use shapes to convey meaning as their ancestors did on cave walls. When mixing powder paint, children are following an ancient tradition of adding liquid to pigment to make colour. Art has always been a vital means of communication for the individual. In guiding children as they develop the skills needed to use the full range of art materials in the primary school, the teacher is helping them to develop the power to express thoughts, emotions and ideas using their imagination, memory and powers of observation. Rather than dismissing art as a lightweight area of the curriculum we need to recognise its potential as a profoundly intellectual activity.

It is easy to understand the temptation to teach art by coaching children in a way that will produce immediate, measurable results which show evidence of knowledge acquired about 'great' artists, rather than to take the necessary time to create rich, diverse experiences that involve the individual child in critical, creative thought that is not so easily measured, but is of lasting value. Some schools have resisted the 'quick fix' temptation, and the following case study is an illustration.

Case study

Sandiway Primary School, in Cheshire, has found that it is possible to set high standards without sacrificing the child's rights to stimulating experiences, opportunities to make decisions about work in progress and time to complete and reflect upon their tasks. The school has a history of valuing creativity in the curriculum and this is firmly embedded in the school's philosophy and practice. The school uses a thematic approach as a vehicle for learning. Creativity is planned for explicitly, and children's thinking skills are developed across the curriculum, including the visual arts. In the academic year 2001/2, the school analysed its approach to creativity as part of a self-evaluation. The starting point was to arrive at a shared definition of creativity which could be included in the school's statement of philosophy and practice:

Definition of Creativity
Imaginative activity fashioned so as to produce outcomes that are both original and of value. (National Advisory Committee on Creative and Cultural Education (NACCCE) 1999: 29)

Creativity is a transforming experience which happens when:

- there is independence of thought;
- thinking is unfettered and imaginative;
- new ideas are generated and developed;
- curiosity is aroused;
- the spontaneous is valued and developed;
- something unique is expressed (in whatever form);
- something new or special emerges.

This is not a definitive list, nor do all the ingredients have to be present for creativity to occur.

(Sandiway Primary School Policy 2002)

As Crace (2002) stated, creativity is difficult to measure and quantify yet there is pressure in schools to do just that with all areas of the curriculum. In order to explore how creativity might be evaluated and to think about cross-curricular links, the school developed an observation proforma (Table 7.1).

Table 7.1 Observation proforma

Points for observation	Seen by:	Comments
Questioning: – open ended – challenging – generating ideas		
Thinking: – imaginative – searching for alternatives – innovative ideas/outcomes – lateral rather than linear		
Responses: – children absorbed/excited – ideas extended – valued by teachers and other pupils – willingness to take risks – independent decision making		
Opportunities: – to use a range of senses – for collaboration – for individual responses – for reflection and review		

The proforma allows the teacher to monitor the teaching and learning process over a period of time using a structured framework to observe, record and analyse opportunities for, and outcomes of, creative thought and activity. Clement *et al.* (1998), Moyles (1990) and Peter (1996) have all stressed the importance of monitoring children's achievement and progress in art and creativity. Moyles (*ibid.*: 123) reminds us that 'the epitome of good records is brevity with clarity and depth' and cites Shipman (1983: 74), who warns that 'the time devoted to completing them [school records] is rarely matched by the time spent consulting them'. The proforma is flexible enough to allow the teacher to make brief comments or more in-depth comments about a range of points without demanding the laborious ticking of boxes which can provide a mass of dense but relatively useless material. We have shown two examples of whole-school policy on creativity. We now turn to the work of one of the classes for a more detailed account of practice. The Year 2 teacher is also the school's deputy head and her practice, as described below, is typical of practice seen throughout the school. First, she describes some of the essential ingredients that underpin her enthusiasm for visual art (the examples that the teacher describes of the work on rhododendrons are explained in detail after the interview transcript).

Ivy: What is it that excites you about the visual arts?

Helen: I love teaching art. It is a really satisfying experience that allows both the teacher and child to learn together. I am very fortunate to be in a school where the visual arts are promoted and time for teachers to experiment with new concepts and materials is encouraged. I think the visual arts probably allow more autonomy for teachers in the planning and delivery of the curriculum, and so they are a more satisfying experience at a personal level. Children and teachers are able to make mistakes and get messy! It is also a time when teachers and their young pupils can relax and enjoy learning together. For example, after a visit to a working corn mill, I took all the children in the hall for the day and, with parental support, the children produced large paintings of the machinery using photographs taken on site. The children were calm, quiet and relaxed and itching to return to the art work. They arrived with their parents at the end of the day to admire their results. In art, although we may have an end result in our 'mind's eye', for the children there is no right or wrong answer and therefore they are more likely to succeed. I have observed children with low self-esteem because they struggle daily in numeracy or literacy. In art they often succeed according to their own strengths and abilities and this is exciting and rewarding. I find it so inspiring to develop an idea with young children that begins with a single thought or picture, often spontaneously and then grows into a project that produces high-quality work. The reward for the child who watches the finished painting or clay model being displayed is most satisfying.

Ivy: What is it about the visual arts that particularly contributes to the development of creativity?

Helen: There are so many features of creativity that are developed within the visual arts. When children are engaged in the process of drawing or painting, for example, they are using their imagination to produce an end-product that is original to them. They will not have produced exactly the same result before and will not replicate the work again in exactly the same form. When I watched one of the children pick up the marker pen and draw the rhododendron I realised that she was using her imagination and was involved in mental play. The result that the child generated was original. I think the visual arts offer children experiences and opportunities that are of real value and have a clear purpose that is relevant to the child at that time. For example, the rhododendrons were growing outside the window and the children admired them. One child suggested we could draw them and display the pictures in school. This process allowed the children to feel valued and there was a real intention. The visual arts allow focused experimental activity and encourage an attitude towards creative learning – a sense of excitement and wonder, curiosity, respect and optimism. By teaching the visual arts, we encourage self-expression on a given task. For example a child who is building a ceramic tile will be encouraged to develop his or her own ideas and make choices regarding the design and tools to use. Finally, the visual arts allow children to take risks, encourage them to question and to find solutions to problems in a secure environment.

Ivy: What problems do you envisage in a primary school which might constrain you in your beliefs about practice in the visual arts?

Helen: It is absolutely essential that the head teacher, governors and parents support and promote creativity and the visual arts as part of the ethos and philosophy of the primary school. Those running the school should be confident in ensuring that the vision for the school includes a wider educational perspective than levels of achievement in SATs and the target-setting process. Only then can the teaching of the visual arts make a significant contribution and be successful. A respectable proportion of the budget will be spent accordingly on good quality resources. Continued professional development will be encouraged in all staff and the art co-ordinator's role will be respected. Without this active promotion of the art within the school, the curriculum will become narrow and time for the development of the arts will be minimal. The local education authority, in turn, should endorse the arts and provide opportunities for teachers to train, exhibitions to run and educational visits to continue as well as sustaining good quality resource centres. I would like to see local education authorities responding to the issue of promoting creativity, a national priority, and returning enjoyment and excitement to the primary curriculum.

During the summer term of 2002 investigation of the local environment was the starting point for work in art, geography, history and science. Rhododendrons grow immediately outside the Year 2 classroom window and provide the habitat for some of the wildlife for observation and study. The children, who are used to making decisions about the direction their work takes, decided that they wanted to paint some large pictures of the rhododendrons. The process involved three stages: observation of the plants; detailed sketchbook drawings; and individual children's decisions whether to paint the whole plant or focus on one flower.

The importance of children using drawing to explore, make sense of and understand the subject being studied cannot be over-emphasised and the process of drawing enabled them to make decisions about how the work was to develop. In this instance they were making decisions within a context, the parameters of which had been defined by the teacher in consultation with the children. Schiller (1979: 76) argued that: 'to be creative one must exercise personal individual choice not only in deciding what, but also each part, each element of what is created'. However, he adds the caution that: 'To give children opportunity for choice beyond their capacity to choose is always foolish, and it can be disastrous'. The experience of making decisions helps children develop the skills needed for taking responsibility for their learning.

After the children had drawn the rhododendron flower they were asked what the next steps would be. The aim was to involve the children in the planning and decision-making for continuing activities. They created a comprehensive list of activities such as printmaking, collage, textiles and clay. They also produced a list of the tools and materials necessary for their chosen activities, which included brushes, watercolour and acrylic paint, chalk, oil, pastel and paper or card. The children elected to begin painting the rhododendron flower using their original sketches. They were keen to produce large paintings to display in school, as in an art gallery, 'so that we can share our work and be proud of the paintings we have worked hard on!' Another child expressed the opinion that displaying their work 'helps us to feel like one big family'. The children chose A2 card, a range of brushes, acrylic paint and pastel for their paintings, drawing the shape of the whole plant or single flower with a big black marker pen (see Figure 7.1)

In order for the children to make diverse choices they needed a wide variety of previous experiences and examples to provide a 'store' of skills and activities. In preparation for this the class teacher used the local Education Library Service to gather art books, and her own personal research using the internet at the planning stage allowed the children access to a wide range of examples that reflected the life and work of the American artist Georgia O'Keeffe (1887–1986) whose work seemed to chime well with the subject of rhododendrons. The high quality of the colour plates meant that the children were exposed to the best

Figure 7.1

possible reproduction of O'Keeffe's images. The children's curiosity was aroused and their thinking skills were developed by the teacher asking and responding to open-ended questions about the paintings.

The children were involved in the evaluation of their own work, something they had done regularly before. They used a Polaroid camera and digital camera to photograph some of the paintings of the rhododendrons. The photographs were used in subsequent plenary sessions to evaluate with the children what they had achieved and to assess how they had used their imagination. Part of the normal process of any project in Sandiway is the engagement of the children in critical analysis. In this case, and as part of the process of making decisions about continuing activities, the children were asked to consider the following questions:

- Why are we doing this?
- What is creativity?
- What is your imagination?

The following are examples of the children's responses:

Why are we doing this?
The children thought the work was interesting, exciting and adventurous. They also thought it was fun. The classroom environment was very important for them. They wanted to see some large paintings in the classroom. The children liked to see their work exhibited because it made them feel proud, pleased and part of a family.

What is creativity?
The children thought that creativity involved making something new for them-selves and others. This might be a new idea, not necessarily a made artefact. Use of the imagination was essential to this process.

What is your imagination?
One child defined imagination as being something unseen in the brain. Another saw it as a little box in the brain that had to be opened for new ideas to come out. Certain conditions were identified by the children as being necessary to facilitate the use of imagination. These included: time to think; a quiet place to think; and the freedom to look as though they were daydreaming. One child said, 'You might need to be doing something else at the same time, like watching television, reading a book or listening to music'. These seven-year-olds were identifying criteria similar to those reached by Steers:

> Serendipity often plays a key role in developing creative outcomes and it is dependent on more than just good luck or fortune. It requires 'space', of a kind in short supply

in target-driven schools, to allow for making happy and unexpected discoveries by accident or when looking for something else.

(Steers 2002: 3)

Following completion of their paintings the children pursued a number of related activities that were cross-curricular. A printing workshop was set up and the children explored printing on fabric using polystyrene and printing inks. They investigated 3D model-making using clay to produce individual terracotta tiles based on their original sketches. Further use of ICT was made by using the drawing package 'Colour Magic' to replicate the paintings and link the children's learning to numeracy by investigating symmetry and tessellation.

It can be seen from the practical examples above that the statutory requirements for 'exploring and developing ideas' (1a, 1b) of the programmes of study at KS1 (DfEE/QCA 1999: 16) were being met. Discussion, questioning and answering were important features of this process. The requirements for 'investigating and making' (2a, 2b, 2c) were being met as pupils developed their initial sketches and information to make paintings, prints, collages and models. These activities involved exploring and gaining mastery of a range of materials, processes, tools and skills, including drawing, printmaking, etc. All the visual elements of line, tone, shape, colour, pattern, texture, form and space were addressed. Pupils were continually exposed to, and encouraged to use, this visual vocabulary in order to review what they had done (3a) and to identify what they might change and develop (3b). In planning for children to engage in evaluating and developing their work in this way the teacher was meeting the statutory requirements and involving the children in the assessment of their work.

If we are to develop creativity in children, as teachers we need to be creative ourselves and be prepared to take risks. We need to create an environment in which children feel that it is 'safe' to 'fail'. We need to know that art and the intellectual challenge which it can offer encourages children to think, to make decisions and to make choices. It enables them to develop knowledge about the works of others and to develop the ability to be articulate and self-critical. It takes commitment and vision to create this environment and this is not easy in a contemporary educational climate that relies on a common curriculum, centrally imposed initiatives and a heavy inspection regime. The reason that some schools, like Sandiway, are able to achieve creativity through the visual arts can also be seen in the further reflections of the teacher.

Ivy: Creativity in art is obviously of central importance to the school's philosophy. How did you identify the skills and qualities a teacher needs to be able to plan for, monitor and assess creativity?

Helen: I took part in a DfES Best Practice Research Project. My investigation explored aspects of the development of creativity. I wanted to identify the

Ivy: skills and qualities you just described and to see how they could be transferred to all curricular areas.

Ivy: What were your main conclusions particularly regarding art?

Helen: The teacher must be willing and able to listen to children and to devolve some responsibility to them.

Ivy: The basic right to mix their own paint, for example, as well as make more sophisticated decisions about how their work will develop? You gave some examples in the case study when children were deciding whether to make large paintings first or prints based on their initial drawings.

Helen: Yes. This also implies the teacher's need to invest time and space to allow thought and ideas to develop. It emphasises the need for the teacher and learner to be flexible in exploring the unexpected.

Ivy: The skills and visual elements defined in the Programmes of Study of the National Curriculum order for art are accessible for teachers. The document is straightforward enough to enable teachers who doubt their own curriculum knowledge to access a framework within which to work. Do you think staff-development sessions are a good idea to develop exciting ways of working within this framework?

Helen: Yes. It's very important for teachers to try to develop a positive attitude to the development of their own skills as artists so that they can enjoy working alongside the children.

Ivy: I have always found it fascinating to work alongside children in the knowledge that I would be learning as well as they. Visiting local galleries and museums, visiting websites, focusing on the work of one artist with all the cross-curricular possibilities that go with that can be really exciting. Also, current events and issues can provide a good starting point for discussion; the *Madonna of the Pinks* for example. As well as discussing the picture in terms of colour and mood etc., think of exploring why the picture was painted, what was happening in the world at the time? That could lead into following the picture on its journey to Northumberland, discussion of the ethics of ownership . . .

Helen: . . . which brings us back to skills and qualities needed by teachers, a crucial one being the ability to be creative in planning so that curriculum areas are enriched and supported by links across the subjects, and activities are open-ended so that the imagination is developed and creativity is nurtured.

Ivy: And, of course, the ability to organise and manage the classroom so that materials are of a high standard and children understand how to use them.

The children at Sandiway Primary School are benefiting from a creative environment where all these conditions apply. The time invested in questioning, thinking about and analysing processes, as described in the case study, is time well spent when it results in children being able to understand what they are doing, and why they are doing it, and then being able to take some responsibility for future directions and development.

The National Curriculum (DfEE/QCA 1999: 16,18) makes explicit the visual elements which comprise the language of art. These are line, shape, tone, texture, pattern, colour, form and space. Teachers need to share with children an understanding of these terms so that a meaningful dialogue about visual art can take place and ideas and perceptions be shared. One way to achieve understanding, familiarity and fluency with these terms is to use them to engage with the work of a range of artists from varying cultures and times. In everyday life, the terms can be used to analyse and describe changes in the tone and colour of the sky, the texture of tree bark, the shapes and patterns of nature, the form of stones and pebbles, the way buildings relate to each other in the space they occupy, and so on. These discussions are translatable to landscapes, still life, narrative pictures, abstract pictures, textiles, and so on.

This chapter has argued that creativity is difficult to define and teach because it embodies attitudes and ways of seeing rather than facts to be learned. Children's ability to be creative in art is facilitated by their acquisition of skills and understanding of the visual elements. This will depend upon a rich and stimulating school environment where a broad and balanced curriculum is assured.

Certain conditions have to be present for creativity to flourish. Children have definite ideas about the nature of creativity and the conditions needed to develop it, and these should be respected and accommodated. Teachers need to understand and respect the importance of creativity and to invest time in ensuring that the conditions necessary for its development are met. Children learn and express understanding in a variety of ways. It is wrong to define a curriculum narrowly and to place emphasis on a few subjects (core) at the expense of others (foundation). The DfEE report *All Our Futures: Creativity, Culture and Education* (NACCCE 1999: 90) delivered a powerful message that is still being ignored:

> Teachers cannot develop the creative abilities of their pupils if their own creative abilities are suppressed. This too has implications for the curriculum – and in particular for the type and amount of national prescription of what is taught and how, and for teacher training. Teaching for creativity is a demanding process which cannot be made routine.

Creative touches

- Provide a wide range of tools and materials that are displayed carefully and that are easily accessible within the classroom. Encourage children to use them.

- Develop your subject knowledge along with the children's.

- Utilise a variety of media, for example: drawing, painting, silk screen printing, batik, clay, etc.

- Design your classroom so that it promotes first-hand experience by displaying interesting artefacts from the natural environment. Use these to stimulate curiosity as well as providing stimuli for children's art work.

- Display children's work as professionally as you can. Look at the ways that professional exhibitions display art work for inspiration. Don't forget informative texts that support these. Work ought to be mounted on neutral colours (black/white/brown/cream) so that the work stands alone and is not distracted by the confusion of multiple colour schemes.

- Give children time to follow through and finish an activity; they need time to experiment and make mistakes.

- Encourage self-expression and be prepared for an end-result that is unexpected!

- Build into your planning some free play with ideas, developing a child's ability to critically evaluate ideas and possibilities.

- Give children choices.

- Plan carefully for continuity and progression using QCA or other schemes of work as starting points. Remember they are not rigid, set 'in stone'.

- Assess children's work in the visual arts as with any other subject.

- Extend children's experience beyond the classroom. Visit art galleries, invite artists into school, set up exhibitions and invite parents in to view.

- Allow for diversity and offer the children a wide variety of experiences. Study art and artists from different cultures and periods of time.

- Encourage autonomy on both sides, a feeling of ownership and control over the ideas that are being offered. Involve children in the planning of activities and choice of tools and materials in the process. Encourage them to mount work and display it with your guidance.

- Above all, have fun, relax and enjoy teaching the visual arts.

References

Clement, R., Piotrowski, J. and Roberts, R. (1998) *Co-ordinating Art across the Primary School*. Lewes: Falmer Press.

Crace, J. (2002) 'Creative spaces'. *Education Guardian*, June 18.

Department for Education and Employment (DfEE) and the Qualifications and Curriculum Authority (QCA) (1999) *The National Curriculum: Handbook for Primary Teachers in England. Key Stages 1 and 2.* Norwich: HMSO.

Moyles, J. (1990) *Just Playing? The Role and Status of Play in Early Childhood Education*. Milton Keynes: Open University Press.

National Advisory Committee on Creative and Cultural Education (NACCCE) (1999) *All Our Futures: Creativity, Culture and Education*. Suffolk: DfEE Publications.

Peter, M. (1996) *Art for All*. London: David Fulton.

Schiller, C. (1979) *In His Own Words*. London: A & C Black.

Shipman, M. D. (1983) *Assessment in Primary and Middle Schools*. London. Croom Helm.

Steers, J. (2002) *Creating Creative Balance*. National Primary Head-Teachers' Association Newsletter.

Tanner, R. (1987) *Double Harness*. London: Impact Books.

CHAPTER 8

Thinking across the curriculum

Carole Mindham

The major concern of teachers is the quality of learning taking place in their classrooms. Children come to us with a wide range of capacities, aptitudes and experiences. A school or class community may at first appear to be fairly homogenous. However, a brief observation of children at work and at play, a short discussion, or an assessment of the end-products of an activity will soon point to significant differences. The positive aspect of these differences is reflected in the particular abilities, capacities and aptitudes which children have and which can be developed with each year of schooling. The negative aspect is the fact that teachers have been forced to differentiate, mainly to improve scores in standardised tests. Often these negatives interfere with the positives.

Great emphasis is placed on children's achievements in maths, English and science; they are comparatively easy to measure. But what about those children who perform poorly in these areas and yet manage to excel elsewhere? Every teacher has met such children; the good teacher will recognise and value every child's skills and abilities and endeavour to move each child forward. This is the rhetoric, but in the busy primary classroom how does the teacher begin to recognise these special qualities and valuable, past experiences? This can only be achieved by talking to children, by observing them when they interact with others, by noting their approach to learning tasks; in short, by getting to know them. By noticing what children are doing, saying and producing, one can make far more valuable judgements and assessments than by merely recording test scores.

'Circle-time' is an example of one strategy that can be used to support better knowledge of the children in the class. In classrooms where circle-time holds a special place, the classroom relationships become focused and mutually beneficial. This is a management strategy which enables the teacher to give the undivided attention to individuals that is so hard to do in the normal school day. Circle-time can usefully be approached in the developmental and systematic manner recommended by Mosley (1997) to provide insights into pupils' lives, opinions, views of themselves and their learning. By recognising and approving children's particular skills and abilities, whatever they may be, we encourage their confidence and, in so doing, enable them to think creatively:

> Promoting creative thinking is a powerful way of engaging children with their learning. Children who are encouraged to think creatively show increased levels of motivation and self-esteem. Creativity prepares them with the flexible skills they will need to face an uncertain future.
>
> (Fisher 2003: 29).

Clearly we must give all children the tools with which to learn and develop while recognising that all-round development involves creative, social and humanistic areas. So where in the curriculum is this to take place? Creativity is often presumed to be located within the arts, but, undoubtedly, a creative act is a complex one in whichever curriculum area it takes place and it depends upon the creator's ability to draw on a wide range of experience, understanding and insight: 'Creativity is not unique to the Arts. It is equally fundamental to advances in the sciences, in maths, technology, in politics, business and in all areas of everyday life' (National Advisory Committee on Creative and Cultural Education (NACCCE) 1999: 27).

Marshall (2001: 116) suggests that creativity: 'Seems to hold an ambiguous place in this country. We appear uncertain as to its value, unable to decide whether it is a good or a bad thing'.

It has been suggested that the major tenets of creativity are:

- the ability to see things in fresh ways;
- learning from past experiences and relating this to new situations;
- thinking along unorthodox lines and breaking barriers;
- using non-traditional approaches to solving problems;
- going further than the information given; and
- creating something unique or original.

(Duffy, 1998: 18)

All of these features are commonplace in Early Years settings. Visit a Nursery class and you will see children using toys, using a range of equipment, using language, adults and peers in order to be creative in a variety of different ways. For example, George, aged 3, was creative with language when, as he didn't know the word 'logs' he described a log fire as made of 'tree bits'. On another occasion he had 'fizzy' feet (pins and needles).

> Beyond their obvious charm, some of these youthful creations are powerfully expressive. There is poetry: a youngster might characterise a streak of skywriting as 'a scar in the sky', a peer will describe her naked body as 'barefoot all over' and, almost without

exception, youngsters scarcely out of diapers will produce drawings and paintings
that, in their use of color, richness of expression and sense of composition, bear at least
a superficial resemblance to works by Paul Klee, Joan Miro, or Pablo Picasso.

(Gardner 1982: 86)

So how can we maintain this lively enthusiasm, this level of imagination, playfulness, resourcefulness and creativity as children move through the primary school? How many Key Stage 2 or even Key Stage 1 classrooms provide genuine opportunities for children to be creative or imaginative? 'Any lesson can develop creative thinking if it involves pupils generating and extending ideas, suggesting hypotheses, applying imagination and finding new or innovative outcomes' (Fisher 2003: 29).

Case study

Esther, a Year 3 teacher, was about to tackle 'time'. She knew from her records and observations of her pupils that only a few of them could tell the time. The concept of time is indeed a difficult one, but she felt sure she could arouse the children's interest and cover several areas of the curriculum. She started by collecting as many different clocks as she could, and the children arrived on Monday morning to find a display of clocks and pictures of clocks. After discussing why we have clocks, and how they may have developed, the children made timing devices, sand clocks, candle clocks and water clocks, and they researched the development of time-pieces. Children's activities included lots of timing (How many hops can you do in one minute? How many times can you write your name in one minute?) and discussions on favourite times of the year in order to extend their understanding of the concept of time.

They went out of school and sketched local clocks and they designed clocks for specific rooms in the house. She read the story of Peter Pan (Barrie 1989) and an abridged version of *The Time Machine* by H. G. Wells (1944), and the children wrote their own time-machine stories. They listened to the 'Clock' symphony by Haydn and composed their own clock music. They investigated the opening and closing times of local shops, the starting and ending times of television programmes and how frequently the local bus service ran. They examined the inside of old clocks and made collages of cogwheels and springs. Alongside these activities, Esther took every opportunity to discuss telling the time, to ask appropriate questions and to provide direct teaching when necessary.

Because the children found the theme interesting and of relevance, they were actively involved in their learning. The majority not only could tell the time when the theme came to an end, they also had a greater understanding of the concept and had developed a range of cross-curricular skills. Pupils had been given opportunities to record their work in a variety of ways. They had produced art, music, models and stories. They had developed reading, writing and research skills. All were successful in some elements of the theme.

The experiences children have in school will influence their attitudes to learning and their belief in themselves as learners. If we can organise the curriculum to coincide with children's interests then they are more likely to develop a positive attitude to learning. They are also more likely to be successful. By involving a variety of tasks and valuing skills beyond those associated only with the core curriculum we enable all children to feel a sense of pride in their achievements.

Gardner's Theory of Multiple Intelligences

The American psychologist Howard Gardner has investigated the wide range of abilities demonstrated by individual people and he stresses the value of not only recognising them but also celebrating them and, in school, catering for these particular skills and differing learning styles. His theory recognises what primary teachers have always known, that children have different strengths and learn in different ways. His theory confirms their observations of individual differences and needs and provides justification for a cross-curricular approach to planning.

He has identified eight areas which he describes as separate 'intelligences' but which work together in an integrated way. He describes an intelligence as the capacity to solve everyday problems and to produce things that are of value to a society. Critics have objected to the term 'intelligences' and suggest talents, abilities or faculties, but Gardner denies that other terms are sufficient. Whatever we call them, they are elements in our genetic make-up, and experiences, societal influences and the opportunities we provide in schools will determine those that are nurtured and those which remain dormant.

The multiple intelligences are described below, along with examples from children's learning.

Verbal/linguistic

This is the ability to use written, spoken or heard language, 'sensitivity to the sounds, rhythms and meanings of words and the different functions of language' (Gardner and Hatch 1989: 6). People who exhibit this intelligence enjoy reading, writing and telling stories. They understand correct use of languages and have good memories for words, names, places, dates and, possibly, trivia. They see things in words rather than pictures. They have a well-developed vocabulary and use language fluently. They may enjoy crosswords and word games. The epitome might be a poet or a journalist.

George, quoted earlier, had developed creative skills in this area. He had been exposed to a wide range of vocabulary and ideas and was able to use his past experience to create the words needed to express himself. Despite the emphasis on formal, carefully structured teaching within the curriculum guidelines, it is clear that this intelligence cannot be fully developed or utilised effectively without an element of creativity. Is there space in the curriculum for developing and valuing creativity within the Literacy Strategy? If the teacher rates this highly enough then he/she will make the space, not only for those who have already developed this intelligence but also for those who may need extra encouragement.

Logical/mathematical

The ability to use inductive and deductive thinking 'to solve abstract problems and to understand complex relationships. Sensitivity to and capacity to discern logical or numerical patterns; ability to handle long chains of reasoning' (Gardner and Hatch 1989: 6). Those who excel in this area are comfortable with numbers and numerically based problems. They recognise patterns and readily categorise and make connections. They may enjoy chess, draughts, strategy games and logic puzzles. The epitome might be a scientist or mathematician.

Maths may not, to some, be seen as a creative subject, but any examination of patterns, of geometry, of problem-solving will reveal the benefit of creative thinking, and the chapter on maths offers insight into the creative possibilities of mathematics as a subject in the primary curriculum. The National Numeracy Strategy is rather more child-friendly and action-based than the literacy version and offers opportunities for children to make choices, to observe, investigate and make deductions:

> Maths equips pupils with a uniquely powerful set of tools to understand and change the world. These tools include logical reasoning, problem solving skills and the ability to think in abstract ways . . . Maths is a creative discipline. It can stimulate moments of pleasure and wonder when a pupil solves a problem for the first time, discovers a more elegant solution to the problem or suddenly sees hidden connections.
>
> (Department for Education and Employment/Qualifications and Curriculum authority 1999: 60)

Musical

The ability to enjoy, appreciate and express using rhythmic, musical elements, 'abilities to produce and experience rhythm, pitch, timbre' (Gardner and Hatch 1989: 6). Musically intelligent people are sensitive to rhythm, melody and pitch and can easily reproduce them. They learn through sounds, patterns and rhythms. They may play an instrument, whistle, sing or hum. The epitome may be a musical performer or composer.

Lazear makes the point that this intelligence may have the greatest effect on our consciousness:

> Just think of how music can calm you when you are stressed, stimulate you when you are bored and help you attain a steady rhythm in such things as typing or exercising. It has been used to inspire our religious beliefs, intensify national loyalties and express great loss or intense joy.
>
> (Lazear 1991: xiii)

Many schools do, of course, value and utilise the creative aspects within the music curriculum and this is an area where many children who may not be high achievers in literacy and numeracy can receive some acclaim and motivation. Charlie provides an excellent example. At first he does not appear to have a lot going for him. His teacher says that he was

> physically awkward, he has poor eyesight and needs to wear an eye patch each afternoon. He is continually in trouble in the playground and seems unable to help himself avoid confrontations. His language skills are poor and he struggles with literacy and numeracy. But, when he came into my class (Year 1) from Reception, he could clap a rhythm back to me (only three out of 23 could do this). He loved music sessions but showed no interest in anything else and told me he wanted to play the saxophone (his dad plays the drums). Now, ten months later he is still struggling with the rest of the curriculum but he takes a lead in any composition work we do. He has plenty of ideas for which instrument and which beat would be best to use and can demonstrate how to use it.

Visual/spatial

This is the ability to visualise the world accurately and be able to recreate one's visual experiences. Spatially intelligent people are able to graphically represent their visual and spatial ideas, to think in images and pictures. People who learn in this way tend to think in pictures and need to create mental images to remember information. They may like to paint, sculpt, draw and will easily read maps, charts and diagrams. They may enjoy films, slides and photographs and are epitomised by artists, navigators, decorators, architects, surveyors and inventors.

> Simon was from an extremely unsettled background, which had inevitably affected his personality and his behaviour. He was most difficult to deal with in his Year 2 classroom, a very unhappy, disturbed child who did not participate in any activity and rarely produced any evidence of interest or involvement. When his head teacher brought his violin to school and played it for the children the effect was startling. Simon became engrossed, fascinated and for the first time wanted to do something. He painted a picture of the violin (Figure 8.1) and, from then on, although it was slow, he began to show progress. A focus for praise and an entry point to learning had been found for him.

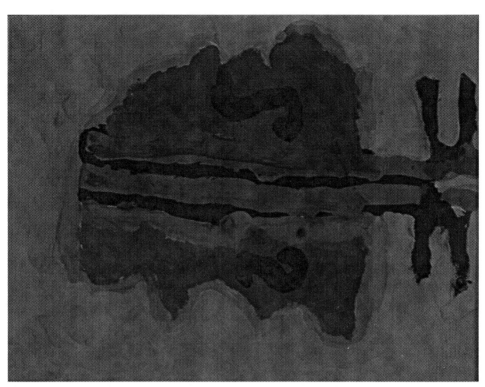

Figure 8.1

Bodily/kinaesthetic

The ability to control and interpret body movements, manipulate objects and establish harmony between body and mind. These people can use their bodies skilfully as a means of expression or they work well in creating or manipulating objects. They have a good sense of balance and hand–eye co-ordination. Through interacting with the space around them they are able to remember and process information.

> People such as actors, clowns and mimes [sic] demonstrate the endless array of possibilities for using the body to know, understand and communicate, often in ways which deeply touch the human spirit.
>
> (Lazear 1991: xiii).

These children learn best by moving around, touching or acting things out and are epitomised by the dancer or the athlete.

> Consider Robert, Year 5. His scores do little to boost the rating of the school and yet he has outstanding ability to organise resources, tools and materials, especially for design and technology activities where he is valued for his ideas and his management skills. Jason, also Year 5, is working at Key Stage 1 levels in both English and maths. His social development is seriously diminished, he is a loner who cannot play,

and yet, as stage manager for the school play he was exceptional. He managed the scenery, the furniture, the props and, when necessary, the other children.

Naturalistic

The ability to observe, understand and organise patterns in the natural environment, to classify plants, minerals and animals. People such as biologists, geologists and zoologists have a highly developed naturalistic intelligence. They are competent in distinguishing, sorting, analysing and ordering taxonomies.

This is the latest intelligence to be described by Gardner. He describes it as:

> The human ability to recognize plants, animals and other parts of the natural environment, like clouds and rocks. All of us can do this; some kids (experts on dinosaurs) and many adults (hunters, botanists, anatomists) excel at this pursuit. While the ability doubtless evolved to deal with natural kinds of elements, I believe that it has been hijacked to deal with the world of man-made objects. We are good at distinguishing among cars, sneakers and jewelry, for example because our ancestors needed to be able to recognize carnivorous animals, poisonous snakes and flavourful mushrooms.
>
> (Durie 2002: 1)

Interpersonal

The ability to understand, co-operate and relate to others: 'capacities to discern and respond appropriately to the moods, temperaments and desires of other people' (Gardner and Hatch 1989: 6). Those who are skilled in this area are usually comfortable with others, try to see things from other people's point of view in order to understand how they think and feel, communicate and negotiate well and may exhibit leadership qualities. Sales people and travel agents, teachers, counsellors and politicians are good examples.

It is easy to recognise among one's own peers the adults who are skilled in this area, but there are also children who show well-developed interpersonal skills. They are frequently those voted as representatives or chosen as leaders in group activities. Cheryl was such a child; in academic terms she was rarely successful but her relationships with her classmates were noticeably positive. She was not looked down upon for her level of achievement because she was popular with everyone – always smiling, cheerful and helpful – and her peers recognised her social skills.

Intrapersonal

The ability to form an accurate model of oneself and to use that model to operate effectively in life, the ability to reflect upon strengths and weaknesses, to evaluate thinking patterns and be aware of inner feelings. Those with a detailed and accurate self-knowledge have well-developed intrapersonal intelligence, they understand their own emotions, know who they are and are realistic about their abilities. They are epitomised by therapists and entrepreneurs.

This intelligence needs careful nurturing as creativity depends upon the process of exploring one's own, very personal, inner world. When circle-time is a valued and carefully considered element in the timetable, children are helped to reflect upon their strengths and to identify targets. Indeed, a positive form of target-setting has become an important task in many schools, and where children are involved in serious and thoughtful consideration of their personal targets and strategies for achieving them, this intelligence can be developed.

> Education concerns itself mostly with learning about the physical world which surrounds us, but we all have an inner world of feelings and emotions which we need to explore, understand and come to terms with.
>
> (Stead 1999: 131)

Gardner (1994) tells us that these intelligences are independent and each has its own pattern of growth and development; different cultural influences will determine which develop strongly, which slightly and which not at all. Each person's profile of intelligence is unique, providing an individual with their own combination of intelligences, which create his or her distinguishable and particular profile.

Despite being aware of individual differences among children, teachers have tended to measure their learning in similar ways and this is reinforced by statutory testing. Such an assumption may work well for those children who are flexible learners, whose learning style matches the teaching style used and those who learn in the traditional, formal manner. But there are those children whose approach to learning does not match the teaching offered who may be well motivated but unable to progress. Gardner's theory offers recognition for such children.

Implications for teachers

Curiosity, being open to ideas and the ability to think about the links between old and new experiences are the key to creativity:

> The avenues through which creativity can emerge are many and diverse. In a classroom context, any curricular area can be the catalyst for its emergence . . . In this view, creativity is not an absolute but a very specific, person-related phenomenon.
>
> (Poole 1979: 9)

Not all children bring the same capacities to the classroom, not all children will learn in the same way and not all children will be stimulated to be creative in the same domain. In order to be creative in any area they must feel confident to build upon their past experience, take risks and try new ideas and resources. Above all they need to feel safe in the approval of their teacher and confident in their own capability. Multiple intelligence theory is not prescriptive. Therefore, teachers are in a very good position to relate theory to their own practice. As children do not all learn in the same way, approaching a topic in a variety of ways will enable more children to be engaged in the learning process, and only through that engagement can creativity be encouraged. Gardner calls this 'multiple windows leading into the same room' (1995: 208). He suggests that every topic should be approached in a variety of ways, that schools should plan deliberately for this by providing a range of resources, both human and technological, 'that fit comfortably with the disparate learning styles and cultural backgrounds that exist in any student body' (Gardner 1991: 245).

To plan learning activities which take account of individual differences, a multiplicity of approaches is needed. They might include:

for linguistic intelligence:

- storytelling and storywriting
- creating idea-maps
- discussions (small and large groups)
- books
- worksheets
- tape recorders
- word processors
- writing activities, instructions, directions, journals
- word games
- speaking and listening

for logical/mathematical intelligence:

- whole-class teaching, questioning
- mathematical problems, calculations, algorithms
- scientific demonstrations, practical work
- puzzles and games, problem-solving, investigations
- classifying
- creating codes
- sequencing, following a recipe

for musical intelligence:

- singing, playing, whistling, humming, clapping
- listening to music, recording music
- music appreciation
- percussion, rhythm, raps
- music software
- creating sound effects

for visual/spatial intelligence:

- charts, graphs, diagrams, maps
- photography
- videos, films, slides
- construction kits
- painting, drawing, collage
- art appreciation
- computer graphics
- optical illusions
- telescopes, microscopes, binoculars

for bodily/kinaesthetic intelligence:

- drama, mime, charades, role play
- gesture, hand signals, signing
- dance
- competitive and co-operative games
- physical awareness exercises, PE
- crafts
- cooking, gardening
- relaxation exercises, stilling

for naturalistic intelligence:

- collecting and organising data
- collecting and organising artefacts
- classifying information
- observing the real world
- keeping notes

- labelling
- identifying and research skills
- observing changes in local and global environments
- caring for pets, plants, gardens
- drawing, photographing natural objects
- binoculars, telescopes, magnifiers and microscopes

for interpersonal intelligence:

- co-operative groups, group projects
- interaction
- board games
- peer tutoring
- simulations
- interactive software
- giving and receiving feedback
- empathy building activities
- community involvement

for intrapersonal intelligence:

- independent study
- individual games, projects
- reflection exercises
- choices
- self-esteem activities
- journal keeping, autobiography, life time line
- relaxation exercises
- self-checking materials

(Armstrong 1994; Fogarty and Stoehr 1995; Wilkinson 1998)

There is one further intelligence to add to this list: emotional intelligence, the extra dimension described by Goleman (1996). He maintains that self-awareness, empathy, motivation and impulse control play a large part in thought and decision-making, and that these can be nurtured and developed. He believes we have two sorts of intellect: the rational and the emotional. The latter matters as much as, if not more than, general intelligence, for if the emotions are not controlled then intelligence cannot work efficiently:

> A view of human nature that ignores the power of the emotions is sadly short-sighted . . . As we all know from experience, when it comes to shaping our decisions and our actions, feelings count every bit as much – and often more – than thought . . . intelligence can come to nothing when the emotions hold sway.
>
> (Goleman 1996: 4)

Within each of these categories there will be opportunities for creativity, for imagination, for making links, for taking that extra step and thinking beyond curriculum subjects. Creativity cannot happen of its own volition or within a vacuum. The famous people we recognise as creative needed knowledge and skill within their fields in order to be creative. Children are more likely to be creative in an area where they are confident, competent and experienced. In order to develop creative children, however, we need creative teachers; teachers who can sustain the creativity of young children rather than damage it; teachers who can be flexible within the structure of the curriculum; who are not afraid to give the scaffolding children need and yet allow for space, time and freedom to take risks and make leaps.

> Creativity thrives when there is time to explore, experiment and play with ideas. To promote creativity you need a questioning classroom where teachers and pupils:
>
> - value diversity
> - ask unusual and challenging questions
> - make new connections
> - represent ideas in different ways – visually, physically and verbally
> - try fresh approaches and solutions to problems
> - critically evaluate new ideas and actions.
>
> (Fisher 2003: 29)

Gardner's theory clearly has implications for primary teachers; he has extended the boundaries of those things which are valued. If children bring with them a range of experiences along with a range of intelligence profiles then the ways in which they learn and the ways in which they will utilise their imaginations are also going to vary. This is not to suggest that we attempt to individualise learning; rather that we consider multiple intelligences when planning; select a range of activities, techniques and materials to engage the majority of children, and thus provide different points of entry into learning.

Armstrong (1994) suggests that once the learning objective is identified then certain questions should be asked (Figure 8.2). Clearly, only some of these questions will apply to a particular lesson or session but if such a broad range of teaching strategies is employed throughout the week then:

> There will always be time during the period or day when a student has his or her own most highly developed intelligence(s) actively involved in learning.
>
> (Armstrong 1994: 65)

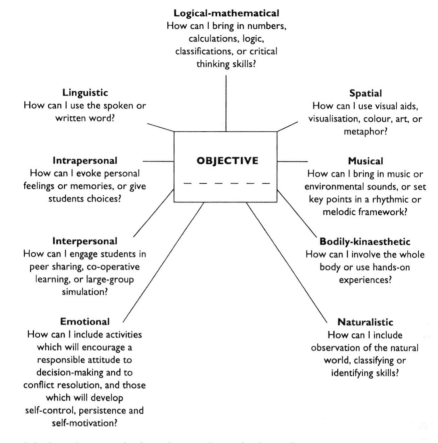

Logical-mathematical
How can I bring in numbers, calculations, logic, classifications, or critical thinking skills?

Linguistic
How can I use the spoken or written word?

Spatial
How can I use visual aids, visualisation, colour, art, or metaphor?

Intrapersonal
How can I evoke personal feelings or memories, or give students choices?

OBJECTIVE

Musical
How can I bring in music or environmental sounds, or set key points in a rhythmic or melodic framework?

Interpersonal
How can I engage students in peer sharing, co-operative learning, or large-group simulation?

Bodily-kinaesthetic
How can I involve the whole body or use hands-on experiences?

Emotional
How can I include activities which will encourage a responsible attitude to decision-making and to conflict resolution, and those which will develop self-control, persistence and self-motivation?

Naturalistic
How can I include observation of the natural world, classifying or identifying skills?

Figure 8.2 Questions to ask when planning for multiple intelligences (Adapted from Armstrong 1994: 58 and extended)

In this way, access to a wide range of experiences will be provided. The ways in which children approach new experiences and new learning will vary according to their past experiences and their intelligence profile. In order to provide opportunities for children to be creative we must vary the teaching approach, provide a range of points of entry and offer opportunities for success. We must allow the child to discover new approaches, to make new connections and to be adventurous. We must give the freedom to work beyond convention. As teachers it is our responsibility to find time to facilitate this process in our classrooms.

We all hope to work with another Masefield, Mozart or Monet and we may just do so. In the meantime we will affect the development of every child in our care. Gardner's Multiple Intelligences provide the theory to legitimise the intuitive beliefs of many teachers. Providing children with appropriate and stimulating activities which build upon their particular strengths or learning styles, giving them some independence, choice and freedom will not only result in deeper learning but also provide the optimum conditions for creative thinking.

Archimedes said, 'Give me a lever and a place to stand and I will move the world.' That's what it's all about, finding a lever, a place to stand, an angle of entry into complexity.

(Waller 1994: 91)

Creative touches

- Consider how you learn – do you like to listen to information or read it for yourself? Do diagrams help? Do you like practical tasks?

- As an adult you probably have an even spread of intelligences but, having completed the record sheet for yourself, do any stand out? Have a notebook with you at all times and make quick notes of any unusual or different behaviour exhibited by your pupils.

- Select between three and five children each day and make a point of observing them during a range of activities. Are you catering for their particular needs, interests and learning styles?

- Try a simple circle-time to establish the listening and turn-taking rules. This can be extended each time you do it.

- Look at the book *Quality Circle Time* by Jenny Mosley (1997). She suggests activities to address self-esteem, self-discipline and positive relationships. Try this one to encourage sharing: the children sit in a circle, they are asked to imagine a friend has fallen down in the playground. What should they do or say? The teacher encourages expressions of sympathy and kindness. The situation could involve role-play of a difficult situation, requiring children to be thoughtful and to empathise.

- Examine a typical week's planning. Which intelligences do you cater for? Could you include different activities to extend the range?

- Could you make some of your sessions more exciting and stimulating by combining subject areas?

- Look at the National Curriculum requirements for next term. Could any of the elements be covered if you plan cross-curricular sessions?

Acknowledgements

With special thanks to the children and teachers of: Cherry Trees Primary School, Lymm, Cheshire; Godfrey Erman Memorial Primary School, Salford; Sandilands Primary School, Northwich, Cheshire; and all the children I have learnt from while teaching in a range of primary schools.

References

Armstrong, T. (1994) *Multiple Intelligences in the Classroom*. Alexandria, VA: Association for Supervision and Curriculum Development.

Barrie, J. M. (1989) *Peter Pan and Wendy*. London: Pavilion.

Department for Education and Employment (DfEE) and Qualifications and Curriculum Authority (QCA) (1999) *The National Curriculum: Handbook for Primary Teachers in England. Key Stages 1 and 2*. Norwich: HMSO.

Duffy, B. (1998) *Supporting Imagination and Creativity in the Early Years*. Buckingham: Open University Press.

Durie, R. (2002) *An Interview with Howard Gardner*. Retrieved 7/8/02 from http://www.newhorizons.org/trm.

Fisher, R. (2003) 'Thinking skills, creative thinking'. *Junior Education*, May.

Fogarty, R. and Stoehr, J. (1995) *Integrating Curricula with Multiple Intelligences*. Illinois, IRI: Skylight Publishing.

Gardner, H. (1982) *Art, Mind and Brain*. New York: Basic Books, Inc.

Gardner, H. (1991) *The Unschooled Mind*. London: Fontana Press.

Gardner, H. (1994) 'Cracking open the IQ box'. *The American Prospect*, 20: 71–80.

Gardner, H. (1995) 'Reflections on multiple intelligences, myths and messages'. *Phi Delta Kappan*, 77(2): 11–14.

Gardner, H. and Hatch, T. (1989) 'Multiple intelligences go to school'. *Educational Researcher*, November, 4–10.

Lazear, D. (1991) *Seven Ways of Knowing*. Illinois, IRI: Skylight Publishing.

Marshall, B. (2001) 'Creating danger: the place of the arts in education policy', in A. Craft, B. Jeffrey and M. Leibling (eds) *Creativity in Education*. London: Continuum.

Mosley, J. (1997) *Quality Circle Time*. Wisbech: LDA.

National Advisory Committee on Creative and Cultural Education (NACCCE) (1999) *All Our Futures: Creativity, Culture and Education*. Suffolk: DfEE Publications.

Poole, M. (1979) *Creativity Across the Curriculum*. Sydney: George Allen and Unwin.

Stead, P. (1999) 'Music', in S. Bigger and E. Brown (eds) *Spiritual, Moral, Social and Cultural Education*. London: David Fulton Publishers.

Waller, J. R. (1994) *Slow Waltz at Cedar Bend*. London: Mandarin Paperbacks.

Wells, H. G. (1944) *The Time Machine ... an Invention*. London: Heinemann.

Wilkinson, D. (1998) *Multiple Intelligence Theory and Teaching – An Introduction*. Oxford: Oxford Centre for Staff and Learning Development, Oxford Brookes University.

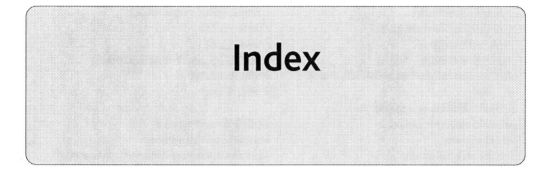

Index

Figures are indicated by italic

Lightning Source UK Ltd.
Milton Keynes UK
25 August 2009

143025UK00010BA/4/A